RAINFORESTS
OF AUSTRALIA

RAINFORESTS
OF AUSTRALIA

EDITOR: PENNY FIGGIS

PHOTOGRAPHY: LEO MEIER

URE SMITH

Four-bar swordtail (Protographium leosthenes)

Project Coordinators: Robert Coupe and Elaine Russell
Production: Gary Baulman
Design and Art Direction: John Bull, Bull's Graphics
Production-Design Development: Cecille Haycock
Endpapers and Chapter Dividers: Leo Meier
Fabric Design: John Bull
Text Editor: Beverley Barnes
Line Illustrations: Susan Tingay

CAPTIONS FOR PHOTOGRAPHS PAGES 1-15

Page 1   Sunrise in Connondale National Park, Queensland.
Pages 2-3   Johnstone River sunset, northern Queensland.
Page 5   Subtropical rainforest tree hosting orchid and fern epiphytes and strangler fig, Lamington National Park, southern Queensland.
Pages 6-7   Morning sun on mist creates a spectacular lighting effect over rainforest at Downey Creek, northern Queensland.
Pages 10-11   A tranquil creek in Lamington National Park.
Page 12   Sunrays beam through the moisture-laden morning air in Connondale National Park, southern Queensland.
Pages 14-15   Rainstorm approaching Lamington National Park in southern Queensland.

Published by Ure Smith Press
an imprint of Weldon International
Level 5, 70 George Street Sydney NSW 2000 Australia

Reprinted 1989, 1992
First published by Weldon Publishing 1985

© Copyright Kevin Weldon & Associates Pty Limited

Typeset in Australia by BudgetSet Pty Ltd
Colour separations in Japan by Dai Nippon Printing Co. Ltd
Produced in Hong Kong by Mandarin Offset

National Library of Australia Cataloguing-in-Publication Data

Rainforests of Australia.

Includes index.
ISBN 0 7254 0803 0

1. Rainforests – Australia. I. Figgis, Penny,
1949-   . II. Meier, Leo, 1951-

574.5′2642′0994

FOREWORD

DR LEN WEBB

Cursed by early settlers as impenetrable 'jungle', 'brush' and 'bastard scrub' and pigeon-holed by English botanists as alien flora from Antarctica and Indo-Malaya, the patches of rainforests in eastern Australia until recently remained aberrant, exotic, and misunderstood elements of the landscape. If the average Australian, apart from the Aboriginal inhabitants, had any affinity at all with the environment, it went no further than the sunny and uncomplicated bush and its hard-knuckled, laconic eucalypts.

To the immigrants stunned by the distances of dry lands and skies, it seemed axiomatic that the strange, even grotesque, flora and fauna had occupied *Terra Australis* since the dawn of time. The dense and gloomy rainforest areas scattered along the moist coastal belt were not only barriers that shouldn't be there, but were also unpredictable when cleared. When dry they burnt well enough, but the rich red and brown earths that supported such a wealth of species often proved disappointing for agriculture. The soils, especially those on slopes and generally with the tallest trees, soon lost their fertility; they eroded and became infested by weeds.

With our widened geographical perspectives today, we know that such failures are common in rainforest areas throughout the world – especially in the tropics – unless there is intensive management and adequate energy inputs such as fertilisers, pesticides and plant breeding. We also know that sustained-yield logging and most plantation monocultures in such situations continue to fail commercially because of economic and ecological constraints. And added to this is the very recent scientific understanding that Australian rainforests are not, after all, alien flora: they and not the eucalypts woodlands bred the aboriginal flowering plants on this continent.

The fate of the rainforests of the world, more than any other natural ecosystem, has highlighted the inescapable need to balance the conservation of nature against the creation of technological ecosystems. We can no longer ignore this need in Australia, where it applies to all our natural ecosystems, most of which have turned out to be fragile. The multi-million dollar question looms large on every Australian horizon: how much longer can we afford (literally, on the bottom line) to damage essential ecological processes? The results are dry or salty deserts, infertile or eroding soils, pest outbreaks, and a degrading human habitat.

Within the last ten years in Australia, the focus of the popular conservation movement on wilderness and especially on the rainforests has become symbolic. These forests are relatively compact, easily separated geographically and in the mind's eye from the baffling immensity of the other landscape problems. As the most favoured and accessible rainforests crumple before the bulldozers, or are impoverished by 'one-off' commercial logging, many Australians now feel we should compare what we have gained with what we have lost. A material question is how much of the cleared lands has remained in a productive and healthy condition, and how much is now unproductive or abandoned? An intangible question, at least in economic terms, is how many native species have become extinct on the moist lowlands and tablelands of eastern Australia?

The time is ripe, and it is not altogether too late, to compare such values – even when the last bottle-trees of once widespread 'brigalow vine scrub' on the subcoastal plains of the subtropics have become like refugees on the horizon; or when the most complex Australian plant communities, on the humid lowlands of North Queensland and northern New South Wales, have been reduced to a few remnants.

Recent scientific evidence has provided fresh and compelling insights about the origins and evolution of Australian biota. The rainforests in what are now our tropical, subtropical and temperate regions represent the descendants of ancient primordial stocks that we shared with India and other countries in the southern hemisphere over 100 million years ago. The eucalypts, acacias, and proteas of the Banksia family that now characterise the Australian landscape were, it seems, derived from ancestral rainforest stocks under special climatic conditions associated with soils of low fertility. The divergence in evolutionary time of these two distinct floras is however poorly understood, and their interrelationships are unique. The survival in favourable refuges (moist, or of high fertility, or protected from wildfires) of the rainforest residues during past periods of aridity seems nothing short of miraculous.

The archipelago of relic rainforests strewn across the Australian continent has within a few years become a classic landscape for scientific research and aesthetic appreciation. It links us in our imagination with the stupendous ecological scenarios of the past. Many of the community types link us with similar types and habitats in tropical and temperate regions elsewhere. Thus despite cultural differences, here are the rudiments of a common ecological language as the result of shared natural resources, and of shared human options for the future in a contracting world.

These new images, and many more as yet dimly seen, have been attained by recent research by relatively few people. Many new avenues should be explored, and more can be opened up in the future to provide new forms and uses of human knowledge. It is therefore clear that the remaining Australian rainforest ecosystems, in their entirety, should be conserved for the benefit of posterity and as an irreplaceable part of the world heritage.

This book is a timely compilation of some of the scientific evidence for the values of the Australian rainforests, and at this stage cannot aim to be definitive. But taken together with the superb photographs, the text should fire the imagination and sharpen the perceptions of all those for whom intrinsic values and the beauty of knowing touch enduring truth.

CONTENTS

Red-necked pademelon caught feeding on foliage
in Lamington National Park.

1
AN OVERVIEW

DR AILA KETO, DR KEITH SCOTT AND ALLAN FOX

T HE RAINFORESTS of the world are nature's pinnacle of achievement on the earth's land surface. Under the closed canopy of a rainforest lies a moist, shaded world of immense beauty, of unsurpassed richness in form and texture. The beauty of the forests is matched only by their importance as the world's richest storehouses of plant and animal communities.

Australia has but a small fraction of the world's rainforests. An estimate of the area of this forest type in the world is difficult to achieve, but it is probably of the order of 10 million square kilometres, or about one and one-third times the size of Australia. Of this, Australia has little more than 22 500 square kilometres, or less than one quarter of one per cent of the total. However, as the chapters that follow will show, the biological importance of Australia's rainforests is very much greater than their size would suggest.

Rainforests have become the centre of a major conservation conflict in Australia. This is a reflection of a rapidly growing concern for such forests throughout the world. Why is it that in recent years an increasingly large number of people have become deeply concerned for the future of rainforests? For many, the reason no doubt relates to the obvious beauty, the majesty of these forests, where nature is at its most luxuriant – the aesthetic aspect that is such an important part of many conservation issues. However, the campaign to protect the rainforests of the world has also been built on the scientific

Red-eyed green tree frog
(*litoria chloris*).

Pages 20-21. Clouds and morning mist surround Cooroo Peak, near Palmerston National Park.

importance of these forests. Indeed, it can be said that the campaign has been led by scientists. Many of the world's leading authorities on rainforests have been trying for years to attain protection of these forests because they fully understand the enormous value of rainforests to the welfare of the planet on which humans are but one dependent species.

THE VALUE OF RAINFORESTS

Scientists such as Dr Peter Raven, one of the world's leading botanists, have eloquently described the values of rainforests, particularly those of the tropics. Tropical rainforests are the earth's richest gene pool on which we depend for our food and pharmaceuticals. These forests are literally teeming with life. No fewer than three million species of plants, animals and microorganisms, of the world's total of more than four million, occur in tropical forests. Only one in six species of organisms occurring in these forests has been described, and named, let alone studied in detail. Yet the forests are being destroyed at an alarming rate. An estimated 250 000 square kilometres of tropical moist forest is degraded or destroyed annually. At this rate, the richest and perhaps most poorly understood global ecosystem will have been largely destroyed within 60 years.

Tropical moist forests have supplied the origins of many of the world's staple foods: rice, millet, cassava, pigeon pea, mung bean, yam, taro, banana, pineapple. This century, genetic resources from tropical forests have allowed breeding of new varieties which have saved a number of important crops, including bananas, ground nuts, sugarcane, cocoa and coffee. The economic value of such operations through use of disease-resistant wild forms has been estimated by the International Crop Research Institute for the Semi-Arid Tropics (ICRISAT) at $500 million (US) annually. Many of the wild and domesticated varieties of crop plants such as wheat, rice, millet, beans, yams, tomatoes, citrus and bananas are already extinct.

New species and varieties are still being discovered. For example, a perennial form of corn discovered in a small patch of montane forest in southern Mexico is estimated to contribute benefits of many billions of dollars annually to the global corn industry. In Papua New Guinea, 251 rainforest tree species are known to produce edible fruit, yet only 43 have at present been brought into cultivation. A protein-rich winged bean from the rainforests of this region is now grown in more than 50 countries. The preservation of the wild gene pool of these plants will be essential for future utilisation of these resources.

Closed canopy of tropical rainforest, Mossman River gorge.

Tropical moist forests are the earth's main repository of drug-yielding plants. They contain the greatest percentage of alkaloid-bearing plants yielding such familiar compounds as morphine, cocaine, reserpine, quinine, ipecac, the vinca alkaloids, ephedrine, atropine, caffeine, nicotine and colchicine.

At least 70 per cent of the 3 000 species of plants that are known to possess anti-cancer properties derive mainly from tropical moist forests. Chances of remission in childhood leukemia have improved from one in five in 1960, to four in five in 1977 because of two drugs developed from the rosy periwinkle, a plant from the rainforests of Madagascar. Sales of these drugs earned $90 million annually.

The rhizomes of *Dioscorea composita* yield virtually the world's entire supply of diosgenin, the parent of a variety of sex hormone preparations including the contraceptive pill. Diosgenin is also the source of cortisone and hydrocortisone used against rheumatoid arthritis, rheumatic fever, sciatica, certain allergies, Addison's disease and several skin diseases. Across-the-counter sales for final products derived from diosgenin total $700 million annually.

The golden bowerbird (*Prionodura newtoniana*), a tropical rainforest dweller.

Hyoscine (scopolamine), used in the treatment of motion sickness and eye conditions, comes from *Duboisia myoporoides* and D. *Leichhardtii*, which are grown commercially in south-east Queensland. There is great variation in hyoscine levels of the different species, which highlights the need to preserve maximum genetic diversity among rainforest plants.

The drug Tylocrebrine, from the vine *Tylophora*, which occurs in Australian rainforests, has proved effective in the treatment of lymphoid leukemia. Other anti-tumour drugs from plants of the Apocynaceae and Rutaceae families are undergoing clinical trials.

The supply of many essential pharmaceuticals is entirely dependent on natural sources. For example, of the 90 medicinal plants found in Africa, Asia and Latin America, 40 are available only from the wild; another 20, though cultivated, are also taken from the wild. Clearly, even though only a minute fraction of the potential for pharmaceuticals has been tapped, we are already very dependent on rainforests for our health and welfare. It has been estimated that there is one chance in four that any medication we use owes its origin directly or indirectly to tropical moist forests. The commercial value of these products together with non-prescription items is of the order of $20 000 million annually.

In addition to these values, there is the more obvious tourist potential of rainforests. To give just one example, the Luquillo rainforest in Puerto Rico was attracting about one million visitors more than ten years ago – people wanting to have a glimpse of tropical rainforest.

Daintree tropical rainforest slopes down to fringing reefs.

Forest reflections in Washpool Creek, northern New South Wales.

It is impossible to discuss the importance of the Australian rainforests without reference to their origins and their history. Our understanding of these aspects has undergone a fairly major revision over the past decade or so. The picture is still far from clear and continues to change rather rapidly, but a number of concepts have now been fairly widely accepted.

About 120 million years ago, the great southern supercontinent of Gondwanaland began to break up, continuing to do so over a period of some 70 million years, and the separating landmasses became the continents of Africa, India, South America, Antarctica and Australia, and such islands as New Zealand, New Guinea, New Caledonia and Madagascar. It is believed that about 100 million years ago, at least the more northern parts of Gondwanaland, including possibly the whole of Australia, were covered with vast forests akin to 'tropical rainforests'. Within these forests were the earliest flowering plants (angiosperms). These plants are thought to have had their origins about 120 million years ago in Gondwanaland. Their development literally transformed the face of the earth as they became by far the most abundant of all plants. Exactly where they originated is still not clear, but a favoured location is the African or northern South American portion of Gondwanaland. There is evidence from studies of fossil pollens that flowering plants were growing in Australia more than 100 million years ago.

Pinkwood (*Eucryphia moorei*) with tree fern understorey, southern New South Wales.

The separation of Australia from Antarctica about 50 million years ago was one of the last events in the breakup of Gondwanaland. The Australian continent then rafted northwards towards the tropics. It appears that at this time the dominant vegetation type was 'tropical' rainforest.

A general global cooling began at about the time that Australia began its northward drift. As will be discussed in Chapter 2, it was the compensating movement into warmer latitudes that preserved the 'tropical' flora in Australia, apparently to a greater extent than in any other part of the world. The global cooling led eventually to the development of cool temperate rainforests in South America, Antarctica, New Zealand and southern Australia. Today, Tasmania is claimed to be one of the world's last remaining strongholds of this rainforest type. The plant species that constitute these cool temperate rainforests must have evolved from the 'tropical' species inherited from Gondwanaland. In this respect, the southern beech *Nothofagus* appears to have been particularly successful, the original 'tropical' type having evolved to produce other species well adapted to both warm temperature and cool temperature climates.

Silhouetted bunya pines, Bunya Mountains, Queensland.

Sunlight glows through misty rain in Dorrigo National Park, northern New South Wales.

Tasmania's deciduous beech (*Nothofagus gunnii*) in winter and autumn.

The picture that has unfolded shows Australia separating from remnants of Gondwanaland about 50 million years ago and rafting into warmer latitudes carrying 'tropical rainforests' that covered essentially the whole of the continent. Associated with global cooling, the climate of Australia became increasingly arid. As a result, the rainforests, which are dependent on a critical level of moisture, contracted to the more favourable areas along the eastern and northern coasts, being progressively replaced by the modern dry-adapted (sclerophyll) flora.

THE PRESENT

The stark statistics are that in the short 200 years of white settlement an estimated three-quarters of Australia's rainforests have been destroyed. The remaining 22 500 square kilometres are scattered and vulnerable.

Today, the remnants of the forests inherited from Gondwanaland survive only as a narrow archipelago of rainforest islands. Although these forests may have been once more or less uniform botanically – because the climate was more uniform throughout the continent – they are now made up of many different types. Like all living things that have ability to adapt to a mix of environmental conditions, the structure of rainforest varies with water, soils, nutrients, drainage, altitude, aspect, light, temperature, wind, seasons, plant and animal associates and evolutionary history. Across northern Australia, with its strongly seasonal climate, are the monsoon rainforests, some surviving tenuously in a few sheltered gorges or moist pockets with springs or seepages. They are probably close to extinction. Along the east coast from Cape York to Victoria and in Tasmania, the rainforest types range from tropical through subtropical and warm temperate to cool temperate. It is worth noting that Australia is the only country in the world where rainforests range from tropical to cool temperate latitudes, giving a unique conservation opportunity.

It has been estimated that there are about 7 500 square kilometres of tropical rainforest (between Cooktown and Townsville in north Queensland), 6 000 square kilometres of subtropical and warm temperate rainforests (from Mackay in Queensland to Eden in New South Wales) and 6 500 square kilometres of cool temperate rainforest (in Tasmania). As well, there are about 2 500 square kilometres of rainforest on Cape York, north of Cooktown, which is a mixture of evergreen and semi-deciduous monsoonal types. Areas of monsoon forests in northern Australia, and of myrtle beech forests in Victoria, are small.

Predictably the plants occurring in the various rainforest types are very different. The great majority of species in tropical rainforests are not found in the cool temperate forests, and vice versa. As stated previously, the highest diversity of plant species is found in the wet tropical rainforests of north-east Queensland. Diversity decreases with increasing latitude. As a result the cool temperate rainforests of Tasmania have 80 species of flowering plants compared with 1160 tree species in the rainforests of the Queensland wet tropics. However, each area has its own unique group of species found nowhere else. For example, 60 of the species in the Tasmanian forests are restricted to them. Areas of cool temperate forest in Tasmania can be dominated by one species, such as the myrtle beech (*Nothofagus cunninghamii*).

Overall, the rainforests of Australia present a bewildering array of life forms and species of both plants and animals. As is the case on a global scale, a large proportion of Australia's flora and fauna is found in the rainforests.

Classification of rainforests – into categories ranging from the complex forests with their two to three storeys, emergent trees, a rich ground and litter layer and a diverse liane and epiphyte flora, to the relatively depauperate monsoon forests of the Kimberleys or Kakadu – has occupied Dr Len Webb, Mr Jeff Tracey, Mr Alex Floyd and other scientists for a lifetime. Anyone with the interest to study the literature will be rewarded with an appreciation of the extensive, difficult and yet elegant work of these dedicated people.

In order to make this book accessible to non-scientists, broad categories have been used:

TROPICAL RAINFORESTS: the most complex and highly developed rainforest types, found from Cape York to Mackay in Queensland.

MONSOON RAINFORESTS: depauperate forests found across the Divide in northern Australia on lands under the influence of the 'summer' north-west monsoon; they occur chiefly in the Kimberleys and the Top End, including Arnhem Land, with patches on Cape York.

SUBTROPICAL RAINFORESTS: the tall rainforest communities found on rich soils, despite rainfall and temperature decline southwards from the tropical rainforests; they occur from Mackay in Queensland to southern New South Wales and include the 'McPherson-Macleay Overlap'.

WARM TEMPERATE RAINFORESTS: forests similar to subtropical, but distinguished by less diversity of species and a simple structure. They occur in patches along the eastern Divide of New South Wales with smaller areas in Queensland and Victoria.

COOL TEMPERATE RAINFORESTS: forests dominated by beech (*Nothofagus*) or pinkwood (*Eucryphia*) in New South Wales; they have their heart in central and south-western Tasmania, with relict outliers as far north as the McPherson Range.

DRY RAINFORESTS AND OTHER UNIQUE RAINFORESTS: unusual 'dry' rainforests which are strongly influenced by seasonal factors, littoral rainforests which occur on the hind dune areas of beaches, and gallery forests which survive along rivers. The forests of the Australian territory, Christmas Island, are included in this category.

HUMAN USE OF THE RAINFORESTS

The first humans to inhabit Australia were people very used to living in a monsoon climate. These coastal people probably made a number of one-way voyages across the 90 kilometres or so of oceanic barrier some 50 000 years ago, taking up residence along the coast and later moving inland. Any effect they had on the rainforest was incidental. In the monsoon areas, the rainforest would supply food for at least half of the year: fruits, honey, flying-foxes, and the starchy storage roots of a number of vine species. Elsewhere, the tendency was to live in the more open forests or on the beaches and heathlands and to move into rainforest for special food known to be there. Aboriginal use of fire may have played a significant role in limiting the spread of some rainforests, particularly into the monsoon savanna areas. Certainly in more recent times the mosaic burning of the monsoon areas over a period of seven months ensured that the huge conflagrations of the late dry season sparked by storms could not occur. Large fires would certainly have pushed deep into some monsoon forests and overridden small patches. While conservation management may not have been a conscious activity, the consequences of Aboriginal living tended that way because of the Aboriginal lifestyle and culture.

The size of tribal units was small and was dictated by the carrying capacity of the land. Aborigines did not apparently kill or destroy for recreational purposes, nor did they have the technology for large-scale destruction. In addition, their cultural ties to plants, animals and the landscape, which had evolved over countless generations, were profound. Their rites and ceremonies emphasised nurturing and protecting the environment rather than conquering it. All this changed with the coming of Europeans, whose attitudes to the land and its creatures were the antithesis of Aboriginality.

At the time of European settlement there was probably about four times as much rainforest as there is today. It was cleared largely because it grew along the more hospitable coastal region where the land seemed most suitable for agriculture and the population was concentrated. So the lowland and plateau rainforests disappeared or were seriously modified, lowlands first, plateaux later – Illawarra, Hunter, Hastings, Macleay, Clarence, the 'Big Scrub' of the Richmond, Burnett, Herbert, Tully, Mulgrave, Barron and Daintree lowlands; Robertson, Coricudgy, Maleny, Comboyne, Dorrigo, Springbrook, Beechmont, and on up to and beyond the Atherton Plateau.

It was also heavily logged for such highly prized cabinet timbers as red cedar, commonly known as 'red gold'. Stories abound of red cedar being used for fence posts, 'out-houses' and piggeries. When only cedar and pine were considered of value, 'useless' timbers such as black bean and white beech were simply burned.

Bar-shouldered dove (*Geopelia humeralis*), Bunya Mountains.

Huge tracts of rainforest have been completely cleared. The 'Big Scrub" in northern New South Wales, the largest area of lowland subtropical rainforest in Australia, was almost completely cleared by the end of the nineteenth century. On the Atherton Tableland in north Queensland, 76 400 hectares out of a total of 79 000 hectares were cleared within a few years. As recently as 1964, 16 480 hectares of lowland tropical rainforest in the Tully River Valley were cleared by American pastoralists for the King Ranch venture, which was economically unviable. It is understandable that the early settlers of these rainforest areas thought there was an essentially unlimited expanse of 'scrub', which was either useful for its logs or an inhospitable obstacle to development.

There seems little doubt that the struggle to save what remains of the Australian rainforests will continue for some time to come. It has already had some emotional peaks, with confrontation between the various protagonists in areas such as Terania Creek and Mt Nardi in New South Wales, Mt Windsor Tableland and Cape Tribulation in Queensland, the Franklin River in Tasmania, and Errinundra Plateau in Victoria. Some of the exploitative uses of rainforest areas, such as the residential development occurring in lowland tropical rainforests in north Queensland and clear-felling for paper pulp in Tasmania, are clearly disastrous. The proponents of the more 'conservative' uses, such as logging, claim that they can extract timber from our rainforests without causing any significant change to them. Conservationists disagree, arguing that these forests are far too valuable to be seen just as a timber resource, especially when much of that timber is used for purposes where substitutes are readily available. The use of rainforest timbers for such purposes as concrete form-boards is inexcusable. Conservationists argue that Australia is in a unique position with respect to other countries where rainforests occur; we are a sufficiently affluent nation not to need to exploit our rainforests and should be setting an example to the rest of the world. There is still time to rescue some of Australia's islands of rainforests. The wisdom of the decision we make about the future of our rainforests will very much depend on the community's understanding of their value.

Rose robin (Petroica rosea)

2

TROPICAL RAINFORESTS

DR AILA KETO

MORE than any other forests in the world, the tropical rain-forests of north-east Queensland are a living link with the vast forests that grew about 100 million years ago in the great south-ern supercontinent of Gondwanaland. As described in Chapter 1, when the continent moved into the tropics the climate became prog-ressively drier and rainforests disappeared from all but a small frac-tion of the land surface. Today, rainforests cover only about 22 500 square kilometres or one quarter of one per cent of the continent.

The largest single block, representing about a third of all Australia's rainforests, occurs in the tropical region between Towns-ville and Cooktown. Not only is this the largest remaining fragment of those ancient forests, but it also has the greatest concentration of plants and animals that are relicts from that era.

LOCATION

Forests that conform to the conventional image of lush and diverse tropical rainforests form the core of about 7500 square kilometres of rainforest which occurs along the coastal strip between Townsville and Cooktown. Most of this lies in the 'wet tropics' between Ingham and Cooktown. Although the rainforest occurs as a more or less continuous tract, two distinct blocks are separated by a narrow ecological barrier north of Cairns, sometimes called the Black Moun-tain corridor.

TROPICAL RAINFORESTS

Most of the northern block, contained in what has been called the Greater Daintree region, is relatively inaccessible. The coastal strip between the Daintree River and Cape Tribulation can be reached from Mossman. Also from this township, the Mossman Gorge National Park at the southern end of this block is readily accessible.

The larger and more diverse southern block, which centres roughly on the Bellenden Ker Range, is accessible from many points. Two routes to the Atherton Tableland pass through this rainforest block and provide views over the area. The southern route to the Tableland from Innisfail, the Palmerston Highway, passes through the narrow Palmerston National Park and provides views of some of the most spectacular gorge scenery in Australia. This highway also provides access to the Downey Creek rainforests.

Forest Structure

Although the rainforests in this region form essentially continuous forest cover which mantles the coastal ranges and eastern escarpment, the appearance of the forest changes very noticeably as one moves from place to place. The changes relate very strongly to moisture and temperature gradients, spatially and seasonally. The effects of wind, soil type and drainage are also important.

Optimum development of rainforest on the globe occurs where rainfall is uniformly high throughout the year with more than 2500 millimetres falling annually, and where temperatures also remain relatively constant and warm. These conditions are more characteristic of the wet equatorial regions. However, parts of north-west Queensland marginally qualify in meeting these conditions which enable the growth of what is called 'tropical rainforest'. Total annual rainfall is certainly adequate, matching the wettest regions on earth. However, more than 60 per cent of the total annual quota falls within just four months of the year from December to March. The distinctly seasonal conditions, despite the high total rainfall, mean that there is nothing in Australia to match the luxuriance and diversity of rainforests in equatorial regions such as Amazonia, Malaysia, Costa Rica, and so on.

The most luxuriant rainforests occur only in the wet tropics, accounting for almost 14 per cent of the major continuous rainforest massif that exists between Cooktown and Townsville. When one considers that Australia is the driest continent on earth, where 80 per cent of the country experiences no rainfall at all for three months of

Pages 36-37. Rattan canes of the lawyer vine palms (*Calamus* spp.).

Morning mists in rainforested gullies, Downey Creek, northern Queensland.

Fallen canopy tree boughs accumulated by wet-season floods.

An ancient tree towers over newly germinated seedlings.

The common tree snake
(*Dendrelaphis punctulatus*).

the year, it is remarkable to find anything resembling the lush, multi-layered tall forests of the humid tropics of south-east Asia and South America.

The presence of tropical rainforest in north-east Queensland becomes even more remarkable when we realise that most of the Australian continent, with an area of 7.68 million square kilometres, was once clad with rainforests akin to these. Fossils of leaves characteristic of tropical rainforest trees, some with characteristic drip-tips, have been found at Maslin Bay in South Australia and date back about 45 to 50 million years. They leave no doubt as to the more widespread occurrence of a 'wet tropical' flora. Conditions then appear to have been warmer and wetter than at present, with rainfall evenly distributed throughout the year.

The warm and relatively equable conditions of the ancient environments existing in Gondwanaland at the time when flowering plants began to evolve and diversify have persisted continuously only in north-east Queensland. So the once-extensive and ancient Australian rainforests, rivalling in size even the present vast expanse of tropical rainforests in the Amazon basin of South America, now survive only as minute relicts.

That they survived at all in the result of a freak coincidence. The global cooling that occurred progressively from about 30 million years ago would have eradicated the warm-adapted rainforests of Gondwanaland were it not for the chance compensating northward drift towards the tropics of the newly separated Australian continent at the time. Therefore our tropical rainforests, although not as expansive or as structurally complex as their equatorial counterparts, are the world's major centre of survival of links with the ancestral forests of Gondwanaland. They are indeed a 'living museum'. The tropical rainforests of New Guinea and south-east Asia, for example, are more 'modern', resulting from the expansion of rainforest into new environments in these equatorial regions.

The survival of the wet tropical rainforests between Townsville and Cooktown has been assisted by the orientation of the mountain ranges in relation to the rain-bearing winds. Almost 70 per cent of what is classified as wet tropical rainforest between Townsville and Cooktown occurs on the foothills and lower slopes of the major massif centring on the Bellenden Ker Range, extending to the Lamb Range just to the north, and to the Walter Hill and Cardwell Ranges to the south. Actual intact coastal lowland rainforest of any reasonable extent now occurs only in the valleys of the coastal streams draining eastwards from the Thornton Peak uplands north of the Daintree River.

In these areas the average annual rainfall is about 2800 millimetres, and the average temperature of 23.9° C does not drop below approximately 14° C during the coldest months. Annual rainfall resulting largely from summer monsoonal storms and tropical cyclones, particularly between December and March, probably reaches 10 000 millimetres or more on Mt Bartle Frere, the highest peak, which has a height of 1622 metres.

A walk into the forest of the lower Downey Creek Valley about 30 kilometres south-west of Innisfail provides a striking but now relatively rare example of intact humid tropical forest of low altitude. It is known as Complex Mesophyll Vine Forest.

Giant trees, some with trunks more than 3 metres in diameter, stand up to 45 metres high with their canopies intermeshed. Below them in the understorey are many other layers of trees, some of which never reach the canopy, while others are the recruits ready to replace individuals in the upper canopy as they die. Some of these forest giants have provided a stable home and source of food for the forest wildlife for thousands of years. One Macintyre's boxwood (*Xanthophyllum octandrum*), for example, with a trunk diameter of 80 centimetres at breast height, has been dated to be at least 3500 years old.

Each layer of trees filters out more of the sunlight, so that as little as 1 per cent reaches the forest floor. The sun-flecked ground can be surprisingly clear and the forest easy to walk through, giving it a cathedral-like atmosphere. Where disturbance has occurred, whether from storm damage or logging, a profusion of vines such as barbed lawyer vines (*Calamus australis*) and stinging trees greatly hamper movement.

Leaves are characteristically large, some exceeding 20 centimetres in length, and often have long tapering drip-tips. The tree-trunks present a great array of textures, colours and shapes. Most striking, and especially common in these forests, are the giant plank buttresses which fan out the base of many of the trees. Thick woody vines are abundant, as are epiphytic ferns and orchids covering the lower tree-trunks and upper canopy branches. Cauliflory, or flowering and fruiting directly from the tree-trunks, is frequently seen. Brightly coloured and often intricately shaped fungi are found amongst the leaf litter, in moist crevices or rotting logs.

It is especially the number of tree layers, the presence of buttressed trees, thick woody vines and epiphytes that gives this forest type the definitive term 'Complex'. Mesophyll leaves exceed about 12.5 centimetres in length.

About 600 square kilometres, or more than 80 per cent, of the

Torrens tree frog (*Litoria nannotis*) clings by sucker-tipped digits.

The palm cockatoo (*Probosciger aterrimus*) of Cape York Peninsula forests.

Complex Mesophyll Vine Forest occur in the foothills of Bellenden Ker Range and the low-altitude reaches of the Walter Hill Range a little further south. Some variation in the basic structural type occurs at higher altitudes or on slightly drier sites. In drier areas such as in the rain-shadow of Mt Bellenden Ker, Complex Mesophyll Vine Forest survives but there are noticeably fewer epiphytes and an increase in the number of deciduous trees. Little more than 90 square kilometres of this variant can be found in the wet tropics, the best development of which occurs along the Mulgrave River.

The Complex Mesophyll Vine Forest described for Downey Creek changes to a simpler structure at higher altitudes, as in very wet areas on the Atherton Tableland. The trees are taller, but leaf sizes of the canopy trees diminish. There are fewer large woody vines, and the forest looks more open and simpler in structure. Only remnants, a mere 120 square kilometres, have survived clearing, the most well known and accessible of this forest type being at Lake Barrine and Lake Eacham on the Atherton Tableland.

It is the mesophyll vine forests that are the only types of rainforest restricted to the tropics. Not all are as complex as those described so far. About two-thirds are classed simply as Mesophyll Vine Forest, in which the number of buttressed trees, woody vines and trunk epiphytes is reduced.

In another variant, at the mouths of the Russell and Mulgrave Rivers in swampy areas with poor drainage, tree palms become predominant. On the soils derived from granite or basalt, Alexandra palms (*Archontophoenix alexandrae*) are the most common. Fan palms (*Licuala ramsayi*) dominate on soils of metamorphic origin. At Hutchinson Creek in the wet lowlands between the Daintree River and Cape Tribulation, almost pure stands of fan palms can be found.

At higher altitudes in the very wet uplands, tree size characteristic of the Complex Mesophyll Vine Forest diminishes, as does leaf size of the canopy trees. Notophylls (7.5 to 12.5 centimetres) and some microphylls (2.5 to 7.5 centimetres) predominate, hence the name Complex Notophyll Vine Forest. Ground ferns, tree ferns and walking-stick palms are common.

Nearby, on soils derived from granites or schists, complexity of the forest changes visibly. Trees are of a more uniform size resembling a 'pole' forest, with trunks mottled grey and white with lichens. Buttressed trunks, large woody vines and epiphytes in the lower storey are rare, although ground ferns and tree ferns are still plentiful. These are Simple Notophyll Vine Forests, the most extensive of the wet uplands. Two-thirds of this forest type occurs on the major rainforest massif centring on Mt Bellenden Ker and Mt Bartle Frere.

Pages 44-45. Lawyer vine, or wait-a-while, suspended over Downey Creek.

Tall and elegant *Archontophoenix* palms.

Macleay's honeyeater
(*Xanthotis macleayana*).

As one ascends higher, both tree and leaf size reduce still further, and the forest is called Simple Microphyll Vine-Fern Forest. At higher altitudes on the windswept granite peaks of the Bellenden Ker Range and further north on the Mt Carbine Tableland, the forests change dramatically to a low dense streamlined canopy no more than 10 to 12 metres in height. Wind-sheared emergents of the *Leptospermum wooroonooran* rise to 15 metres. Some of these trees are thought to be several thousand years old.

FLORA

When the Australian continent finally broke away from the last remnants of Gondwanaland about 50 million years ago and began its northward drift into the tropics, it was carrying a largely unique fraction of the Gonwanan flora. It drifted for some 35 million years without contact with other landmasses. During this period its flora (and fauna) underwent great diversification. As the continent became progressively drier, the sclerophyll plants that now dominate Australia's vegetation developed – the eucalypts, callistemons, leptospermums, banksias and hakeas.

Remarkably, in the rainforests of the wet tropics some of the original Gondwanaland plants still survive today, more or less unchanged. In fact, these rainforests have the highest concentration of primitive flowering plant families of any area in the world. Of 19 families of flowering plants throughout the world that are regarded as most primitive, 13 are found in the rainforests of this region. Two of these are found nowhere else in the world – Austrobaileyaceae and Idiospermaceae. Within the 13 families of primitive flowering plants, there are 50 species that are unique to these rainforests.

Primitive flowering plants in this region include *Austrobaileya scandens*, *Idiospermum australiense*, *Galbulimima baccata*, *Eupomatia laurina* and *E. bennettii*. Professor Peter Endress, a world authority on primitive flowering plants, has described the pollen of *Austrobaileya scandens* as outstanding among living angiosperms for its combination of archaic characters. It closely resembles the oldest known fossil pollen, believed to have belonged to a plant that lived on earth more than 120 million years ago. The occurrence here of these primitive angiosperms, some of the most primitive on earth, is of great importance in that these plants may hold crucial clues that will allow scientists to unravel the story of the origin and spread of the flowering plants which so changed the face of the earth more than 100 million years ago.

Not only have these rainforests of tropical Queensland preserved relics of the original Gondwanaland-derived flora, but they also pro-

Vines, epiphytic mosses and crow's nest ferns, Downey Creek.

A rainbow lorikeet (*Trichoglossus haematodus*) sips umbrella-tree nectar.

Exposed upland tropical rainforest, Daintree coast.

Canopy profile at sunset, Downey Creek.

Downey Creek, home of numerous amphibia and invertebrates.

vide the only habitat for some of the oldest living forms in the evolutionary lines that led to the development of our present-day dry-adapted flora. It is apparent that rainforest plants, extinct or extant, were the ancestors of our existing sclerophyll vegetation. The nearest relatives to those ancestors, if not the ancestors themselves, survive in the tropical rainforests of Queensland. This is particularly apparent within the Proteaceae, a very important family in the Australian flora with such well-known genera as *Banksia*, *Grevillea*, *Hakea* and *Dryandra*. The most primitive genera of the Proteaceae are found in the rainforests of the region – for example, the little-known *Placospermum*, *Sphalmium* and *Carnarvonia*, the first two of which are restricted to the area. These rainforests have apparently acted as a centre of survival for these genera, the oldest remnants of this family. There are 28 species within the Proteaceae that are restricted to these rainforests.

Another connection between these rainforests and the evolution of today's sclerophyll flora is related to the ubiquitous genus, *Eucalyptus*. This genus must also have evolved from rainforest ancestors. Recently, a rare new genus that is thought to be a precursor of *Eucalyptus* has been found at Boonjie on the eastern edge of the Atherton Tableland.

Overall, there are about 1160 species of higher plants (not including ferns, mosses, etc.) in the rainforests of the wet tropics, including more than 450 that are found nowhere else. The species represent 117 families and 560 genera. In fact, about a quarter of all Australia's plant genera occur in these rainforests, accounting for a high diversity at the level of the genus. The diversity at the species level is not so strikingly high, largely because some two-thirds of the genera occurring here are represented by only one species. From a conservation point of view, it is also significant that there are 43 monotypic genera (only one species in the genus) among the higher plants in the area, of which 28 are found nowhere else.

The rainforests of the wet tropics contain the richest concentration of ferns and fern allies in Australia. More than half of Australia's fern species (214 out of 364) are found here, with about 100 species confined to the region. Approximately 15 of these have an extremely restricted distribution, being confined to single locations mainly in the uplands and on mountain summits.

These rainforests also have the richest epiphytic flora in Australia. At least 90 species of orchids are found here, with almost half restricted to the area.

There are also some distinct curiosities among the flora. The area supports one of the world's largest cycads, *Lepidozamia hopei*, growing

A *Nyctimystes* tree frog, a very restricted northern tropical endemic.

to a height of about 20 metres, as well as one of the smallest cycads, *Bowenia spectabilis*, a fern-like plant that is endemic to this area. Another plant of interest is the resurrection plant (*Borya sepentrionalis*) which occurs on mountain summits such as Thornton Peak. In the 'dry' season the leaves of this plant dry out to become a brilliant orange and then rusty brown. Then, after the rains come, it turns vivid green literally overnight.

FAUNA

The tropical rainforest region of north-east Queensland has the highest diversity of fauna of any area in Australia. At least 230 species of vertebrate animals are found in these rainforests, including at least 35 species of mammals, about 140 species of birds, and at least 25 species of frogs and 30 species of reptiles. About 160 vertebrate species appear to be dependent on rainforest for survival. Perhaps related to the high diversity, many species have very restricted distributions, with some confined to just one or two mountain summits. Within most of the groups of fauna, many species are restricted either to higher altitudes or to the lowlands. This is the case within the mammals, birds, frogs, reptiles and insects.

The tropical rainforests of north Queensland represent something of a microcosm of the history of Australia's fauna. Here are not only some of the oldest remnants of lines derived from the stock inherited from Gondwanaland, but also many species derived from the Asian stock that has 'invaded' Australia within the past 15 million years or so. The latter group is well represented in the region within the bats and the rodents.

Numerous species of fauna are shared with New Guinea, and in many cases the region represents the southern limit of their Australian distribution. Some of these species may have come from south-east Asia via New Guinea; others must have been derived from Australian stock, given that New Guinea remained essentially submerged until relatively recent times.

There are no fewer than 54 vertebrate species that are found only in the rainforests of this region. This number is made up of nine mammals, 10 birds, 19 frogs and 16 reptiles. Among these are many of considerable scientific importance – for example because of their position in the evolutionary history of the particular group, or because of their relictual nature, their occurrence here indicating past distributions of their genus and therefore of the rainforest type and environmental conditions on which they depend.

One particularly interesting species of mammal restricted to these rainforests is the musky rat-kangaroo (*Hypsiprymnodon mos-*

The Cape York melomys (*Melomys capensis*), a native climbing rat.

Pages 54-55. Lowland rainforest, coconut palms and fringing reefs at Cape Tribulation.

A tropical beach fringed with lush lowland rainforest.

chatus). The smallest of the macropods, standing only 25 centimetres high, it is in a number of respects the most primitive of the kangaroo group. It apparently represents an early stage in the evolution of the kangaroos from a tree-living, possum-like ancestor.

The most primitive group of marsupials in Australia is the Dasyuroids. The only more primitive marsupials are the Didelphoids (large opossums) of South America. The Dasyuroids, a basically carnivorous group (which includes the quolls, antechinuses and dunnarts), are represented in the rainforests of the wet tropics by nine species, giving this area probably the highest concentration of these species in Australia.

A fading bloom and leaf-litter on tropical beach.

Of the six ringtail possums in Australia, five are found in these rainforests and four occur nowhere else. Australia's only two tree-kangaroos are also restricted to this region.

Dr John Winter, Senior Zoologist with the National Parks and Wildlife Service in Townsville, has suggested that there are two subregions for the distribution of the mammals (excluding bats) in this region. One, the Atherton Subregion, is based on a core-area in the Atherton uplands that is defined by the limits of distribution of the Atherton antechinus (*Antechinus godmani*). The other, the Thornton Peak Subregion, is based on a core-area defined by the distribution of a rodent, the Thornton Peak melomys (*Melomys hadrourus*). These two core-areas are regarded by Winter as centres of endemism for these mammals. Both species that define the core-areas have very restricted ranges: less than 600 square kilometres for the Atherton antechinus and about 200 square kilometres for the Thornton Peak melomys.

The significance of the two subregions is that eight of the nine mammal species that are restricted to these rainforests can be divided into two distinct groups, distributed around one or other of the centres of endemism. Only the musky rat-kangaroo is found throughout the whole region, although its distribution is patchy. Between the two subregions there is a region of overlap around the Mt Carbine Tableland. Because of the overlap, the concentration of species here is high, with a total of 21 flightless mammal species. This is exceeded only by the Atherton uplands, with 22 species.

As noted above, there is a distinct group of mammals that is confined to the upland areas. This includes six of the restricted species: the Atherton antechinus, the green ringtail possum, the two subspecies of the Herbert River ringtail, the lemuroid ringtail and the Thornton Peak melomys. Other species are found throughout all altitudinal zones, with no distinct group of mammals confined to the lowlands.

The rare green python (*Chondropython viridis*) is restricted to the
Cape York tropical rainforests and New Guinea.

Downey Creek mirrors rainforest canopy.

A flowering wild ginger.

Canopy and cloud mist with climbing palms and epiphytic ferns.

A buff-breasted paradise kingfisher (*Tanysiptera sylvia*) takes a green grasshopper to feed its young.

Three species of mammals occurring in the rainforests of the wet tropics show major disjunctions in their distributions. The brown antechinus (*Antechinus stuartii*), which is found in the upland rainforests of the region, is isolated from the main population which occurs along the east coast from south-east Queensland to Victoria. A similar disjunction is seen in the distribution of the spotted-tailed quoll or tiger cat (*Dasyurus maculatus*), one of the largest (body length: to 75 centimetres) and most ferocious of the carnivorous marsupials. The greatest latitudinal disjunction for any Australian mammal is exhibited by the white-footed dunnart (*Sminthopsis leucopus*). The occurrence of this species in the rainforests of the wet tropics has only recently been confirmed. The nearest other population of this species is found in south-east New South Wales, about 2100 kilometres away. According to Stephen Van Dyck of the Queensland Museum, who made the recent discovery of the white-footed dunnart just south of the Atherton Tableland, the species is a relict of a genus that originated in wet forests perhaps 10 million years ago or more.

The birds of the tropical rainforests of north-east Queensland are probably the most diverse in Australia. There are about 140 species inhabiting the rainforests and mangrove forests of the region. Ten species are restricted to the region, the majority of which are confined to the upland rainforests. However, unlike the mammals, there is a distinct group of lowland species. The latter includes the grey swiftlet (*Collocalia spodiopygia*), one of the few echo-locating birds in the world and the only one breeding in Australia. Among the endemic species restricted to the uplands is the golden bowerbird (*Prionodura newtoniana*). The beautiful bird builds a 'twin-maypole bower' up to 3 metres high and 1 metre between the two towers.

Within the tropical rainforests of north Queensland, at least two groups of birds are accepted as having Gondwanaland origins. These are the cassowary and the megapodes (mound-builders). The southern cassowary (*Casuarius casuarius*), a flightless bird standing up to 2 metres tall, is the only cassowary in Australia and one of only three species in the world. Restricted to the rainforests of the wet tropics, the southern cassowary is undoubtedly a relict from a time when rainforests (and cassowaries) were once much more widespread in Australia.

Of the 25 or more frogs that are found in the rainforests of the wet tropics, 19 are restricted to the region. This represents 13 per cent of Australia's frog species. Several species have extremely limited distributions: one tree frog, *Litoria lorica*, has been found only on Thornton Peak; and one of the narrow-mouthed frogs, *Cophixalus neglectus*, has been recorded only from the Bellenden Ker Range.

Two families of Australian frogs may have originated more than 50 million years ago, before the breakup of Gondwanaland. Some of the most primitive species within these families are found in the rainforests of the wet tropics. Of the four species in the genus *Taudactylus* – one of the most primitive groups of frogs in Australia – two are restricted to these rainforests, one of them to three recognised 'refugial' areas, Mt Bellenden Ker, Mt Lewis and Thornton Peak.

Of about 160 species of reptiles that occur on the coastal strip between Townsville and Cooktown, at least 30 predominantly inhabit the rainforests. Sixteen species are restricted to these rainforests. These include Boyd's forest dragon (*Gonocephalus boydii*), the prickly forest skink (*Trophidophorus queenslandiae*), and a skink discovered in 1981 on Mt Bartle Frere and apparently restricted thereto. This skink, *Leiolopisma jigurru*, discovered by Jeanette Covacevich of the Queensland Museum, is another disjunct species, separated from others in the genus by 1500 kilometres. Covacevich regarded the finding of this species in 1981 in the cool temperate habitat on Mt Bartle Frere as the first record of a vertebrate species that must be regarded as a relict from a time when temperate rainforests were continuous throughout, at least, eastern Australia. (There are a number of parallels among the insects.)

Two geckoes occurring in the rainforests of the wet tropics that can be regarded as relict and primitive are the chameleon gecko (*Carphodactylus laevis*) and the northern leaf-tailed gecko (*Phyllurus cornutus*). The former is restricted to these rainforests.

The insects of the tropical rainforests are a particularly interesting group. They show a great diversity and a pronounced altitudinal zonation, some species having a narrow altitudinal range.

The cool, wet upland forests have conserved many primitive insect species that are relicts of the Gondwanaland fauna, with other occurrences of their genera being in distant temperate areas. A striking example is the stag beetle (*Sphaenognathus queenslandiae*), which is found only on Mt Lewis and Mt Windsor Tableland. Its closest relatives are in the Andes of South America. Another is a blind, wingless water-beetle, *Terradessus caecus*, of which the nearest relatives are in the forests of the southern Himalayas. These distributions suggest that both of these species have changed little since the breakup of Gondwanaland more than 50 million years ago.

Terradessus caecus is found only on Mt Sorrow and Thornton Peak, to the west of Cape Tribulation. This area, which is consistently wet, is noted for the presence of terrestrial forms of insects that are normally associated with water. *Terradessus caecus* is one of these.

The Daintree River ringtail possum (*Pseudocheirus herbertensis cinereus*).

Seedlings sprout up between the plank-buttresses of tree-trunks.

Large palm fronds shade an umbrella tree (*Schefflera actinophylla*).

Pages 66-67. Creek beds often afford wider views of dense forests.

A mosaic of fronds.

A rainforest giant, thousands of years old.

Mt Pieter Botte peak, or Nulbullulul, clothed by a colourful rainforest canopy.

Upland tropical rainforest, Roaring Meg Creek Catchment.

A male Cairns birdwing butterfly (*Ornithoptera priamus*).

Tree ferns and other ferns flourish in the lighter areas on creek banks.

Another is a dragonfly, *Pseudocordulia* sp., which is the first recorded example in the world of a dragonfly with a terrestrially adapted nymph stage.

Apart from these species of great scientific importance, there are many beautiful insects such as the bird-wing butterflies and the hercules moth (*Coscinocera hercules*), one of the largest moths in the world, with a wingspan of 25 centimetres.

History of Human Use

Human occupation of the rainforests of tropical north Queensland may date back more than 40 000 years. Sediment cores from lakes on the Atherton Tableland have revealed a dramatic increase in charcoal deposits at about this time, and this has been interpreted as arising from the use of fire by the Aborigines. Indeed, it has been suggested that this use of fire may have contributed to the major replacement of rainforest by fire-adapted eucalypts which took place at that time.

The Aborigines who lived in these rainforests are believed to represent the only rainforest culture to have existed in Australia. The people were distinctive – physically, linguistically and culturally. They developed sophisticated leaching procedures for detoxifying plant foods derived from the forest, such as the fruits of the black bean, Queensland walnut and yellow walnut. The everyday use of these toxic foods distinguished these Aborigines from others elsewhere in Australia.

Aboriginal use of these rainforests continues today, especially in the region of the Bloomfield and Lockhart Rivers. These people represent the last Aboriginal community using the coastal environment in a significantly traditional way, anywhere on the east coast of the mainland. They retain their traditional attachment to the land and the rainforests and continue to use the leaching procedures for detoxifying plant foods.

The mythology of the Djirubal tribe of the Atherton Tableland is of particular interest, in that it describes events apparently associated with past volcanic activity in that area. The Ngadyan legend describes the origins of the crater lakes, Barrine, Eacham and Euramoo. The story tells how the wrath of the Rainbow Serpent caused great winds and twisting and cracking of the earth. The skies were filled with red clouds, the like of which had never been seen before. People trying to escape were swallowed by cracks that opened up in the ground. The story notes that at the time the lakes were amid 'open scrub', not 'jungle'. From the known geological and

The cauliflorous flowers of the black bean (*Castanospermum australe*).

Rainforested mountains produce finely filtered fresh waters, and some rainforests stand on pure sand.

vegetation history, this legend must refer to events that occurred between 10 000 and 15 000 years ago. This appears to be the oldest recorded oral prehistory of any human culture.

Hinchinbrook Island, a strikingly beautiful and interesting area that lies within this wet tropical rainforest region, was the home of the Bandjin Aborigines who constructed complex tidal fish traps using stones cemented together with rock oysters. Extending over 2 hectares, they have been described as unparalleled in view of their size and complexity. They are still functioning today, though they have not been used for a hundred years.

European settlement of north Queensland began in the 1860s. This, of course, meant clearing of rainforest. Dr John Winter has recently estimated that about 2000 square kilometres have been cleared since Europeans arrived. This clearing has most seriously diminished the area of lowland rainforest, such areas being the most suitable for agriculture, especially sugarcane farming. The Atherton Tableland has also suffered heavily, its rich basaltic soils having been found particularly suitable for agriculture and dairying.

In addition to agriculture and grazing, a significant amount of mining has taken place. North of the Daintree River, gold was mined fairly extensively in the past. More recently, tin mining has been more prominent, and this mining remains a continuing source of rainforest destruction, albeit on a relatively small scale.

On a much larger scale, the rainforests have been affected by forestry. Logging began in the rainforests of north Queensland in the 1870s. The early history is one of gross overexploitation and wastage, as was the case for much of Australia's native forests. Whereas forestry practices have improved and logging is carried out under much more strict controls, this industry nevertheless remains the most pervasive threat to these rainforests.

CONSERVATION STATUS

About three-quarters of the rainforests between Townsville and Cooktown occur on Crown land within state forests (51 per cent), timber reserves (10 per cent), national parks (14 per cent) and Aboriginal and Islander reserves (1 per cent). The remainder is either freehold or leasehold land.

The Queensland Department of Forestry has estimated that there are 4441 square kilometres of rainforest within state forests, timber reserves and certain other Crown lands between Townsville and the Daintree River. However, they claim that only 1428 square kilometres are available for logging, the remainder being inaccessible, unpro-

The male southern cassowary (*Casuarius casuarius*) incubates the eggs unaided by the female.

ductive or special land-use areas. This statistic fails to reveal the true picture. It implies that all rainforest is the same, that the forest types in the areas where the terrain makes them inaccessible to logging are the same as those on accessible areas. It also obscures the fact that logging is concentrated in a few rainforest types.

The Forestry Department made no estimate for the area north of the Daintree River, as there is at present no systematic logging in this area because of transport difficulties – crossing of the Daintree River is still via a small vehicular ferry. (There is some logging in the Bloomfield area, carried out within the usual tree-marking controls of the Forestry Department.) However, the Forestry Department has stated that if road access is provided into this area, 'then it would be in the community interest for timber resources to be utilised from any lands which can reasonably be reserved for multiple use forest management'. For this and many other reasons, a bridge across the Daintree River would be nothing short of a tragedy for the rainforests to the north. Such a bridge is the dream of a prominent Queensland Cabinet minister who has 'promised' that it will be a reality within five years.

It is the rarest types of rainforest that have the least protection. Five of these do not occur to any significant extent within national parks. Mesophyll Vine Forest of the very wet lowlands on beach sand, and Notophyll Vine Forest on beach sand, are almost totally unprotected. Complex Notophyll Vine Forest was once extensive on the drier basalts of the Atherton Tableland but has now been reduced to a mere 14 square kilometres with none occurring in a national park. The same forest type on the moister upland basalts is somewhat more extensive, but only 0.6 per cent is protected by national park status. The striking Mesophyll Vine Forest with fan-leaf palms that is found on very wet lowlands with impeded drainage has been reduced to about 5 square kilometres, very little of which is in national parks whereas nearly 60 per cent is on freehold or leasehold land.

At the beginning of 1984 it was estimated that about 2180 square kilometres of rainforest within the region between Ingham and Cooktown remain in a virgin condition. This represents some 42 per cent of the total. The virgin area is, however, continually decreasing. In July 1984, the Forestry Department began logging the last area of accessible virgin rainforest in this region – the lower Downey Creek catchment, west of Innisfail. Virgin areas remain largely at higher altitudes and areas of limited access.

The conservation status of individual species of plants and animals is much more difficult to assess. Such an assessment requires

Coastal cloud moisture sweeps over Mt Sorrow in the Daintree area.

biological and ecological data which are not available. One species of mammal is considered to have a poor conservation prognosis. This is the spotted-tailed quoll, a relatively large carnivorous marsupial. It is thought that the quoll's numbers are being reduced by eating cane toads which are toxic to them. Cane toads, an introduced pest, are essentially absent from undisturbed rainforest but are much more common where roads and logging tracks have been constructed through the forest.

There are many rare and very restricted plant species in these rainforests. Indeed, only about 6 per cent of the higher plant species of the area can be regarded as common. More than 40 species are regarded as very restricted, with 23 species considered to be threatened. One apparently very rare plant is a species of wild banana, *Musa fitzalanii*. It has not been recorded since it was first collected near the Daintree River more than a century ago. *Hexaspora pubescens*, a monotypic endemic tree species, was thought to be extinct until recently rediscovered in a state forest on the western slopes of Mt Bartle Frere.

Threats to the rainforests imposed by logging and mining have been discussed above, but the conservation picture would be incomplete without reference to the most devastating of all – residential development. To anyone who appreciates the value and importance of these rainforests, it is heart-breaking to see the residential development currently occurring between the Daintree River and Cape Tribulation. These precious remnants of tropical lowland rainforest are one of the major centres of survival of primitive flowering plants. To see them being carved into blocks like any suburban development, for the profit of a few developers and wealthy individuals, causes feelings of despair. Given the outstanding universal value of these rainforests, there is a strong case for public ownership of the whole area – and as soon as possible.

The colours and textures of a large palm crown.

Boyd's rainforest dragon (*Gonocephalus boydii*).

White-tailed kingfisher (Tanysiptera sylvia)

3
MONSOON FORESTS

ALLAN FOX

ONSOON is said to have been derived from the Arabic *mausim* meaning season, and if one were looking for a land of distinct seasons, it would be difficult to find a better example than the Top End of Australia. Anywhere from Port Headland to Princess Charlotte Bay, Cape York, is the land of the monsoon . . . the land of the 'wet' and the 'dry', of the 'hope and the suicide season'. The monsoon climate determines the nature of the monsoon forest, or, to be more technical, of the monsoon vine forest.

The continental drift of our land has placed us south-east of the Indian/Indo-China subcontinent, separated by a 3000 kilometre band of tropical sea bisected by the equator, with the Tropic of Capricorn running through Rockhampton. The tilt of the planet creates seasonal bands of intense heating over Asia and Australia in July and January respectively. By December the surface of northern Australia has heated to its maximum, and the hot air mass over it rises, sucking in the saturated air off the warm tropical seas. This north-west flow of air becomes a steady humid wind, the monsoon. Water vapour is lifted by the rising continental air into cooler altitudes, condensation occurs and the intense and steady monsoon rains begin. To complete the circulation and to maintain the atmosphere's dynamic balance, the rising air at high level drains back across the tropics as cooler drier air towards the north-west, subsiding north of the equator to sweep on to Asia maintaining the dry season there. Thus the solar-engine of the monsoon works, reversing

The plumed or intermediate egret (*Egretta intermedius*).

Lowland rainforest with emergent *Archontophoenix* palms, many of which are conspicuously in flower.

when the heated band lies across Asia, creating our dry season – a process that has been working on northern Australia for perhaps 20 million years.

Over the past million years, however, there have been many cold periods modifying the process. Several of these periods were so cold as to cause the sea level to drop a hundred or more metres, shifting the coastline hundreds of kilometres in some places towards Timor and West Irian, greatly reducing the impact of the weakened monsoon. Aridity arrived with the cold, and what is generally open forest today in Kakadu, 16 000 years ago was low open woodland (somewhat like that on the country south of Tennant Creek today), while most of the Kimberley was covered with a shrubland. However, during these arid periods, deeply dissected plateaux and ranges contained damp refuges, where many plants managed to survive. These waves of aridity placed the flora under test, and the survivors had their special survival adaptations strengthened by the test. With the return of more humid and warmer conditions, these survivors were released from their bondage in the refuges of hidden gullies, springlines and southerly aspects. Birds, particularly the pigeons, began the enrichment of the residual forests by disseminating seeds of juicy-fruited species from Cape York. Meanwhile the rising seas encroached on shorelines, flooding coastal plains and river systems.

While environmental stress was pushing the species about and generally reducing diversity, some of these survivor species reproduced in such a way as to consolidate the changes by establishing an endemic species specially able to cope with the local conditions. The end result of all of this genetic sifting was to produce suites of species well able to survive periods of drought and able to disperse readily and to establish themselves. These became essential characteristics for organisms successfully living in northern Australia with its long dry season. One of the clearest examples of this capacity to aggressively exploit ecological opportunities is seen at Victoria, the settlement that was abandoned on Port Essington 146 years ago. The parade ground and vegetable garden, once fully cleared of native vegetation, is now a well-developed, floristically rich, semi-deciduous monsoon vine forest. In the broader time scale, 70 per cent of the obligate monsoon vine-forest flora is found on landscapes less than 10 000 years old.

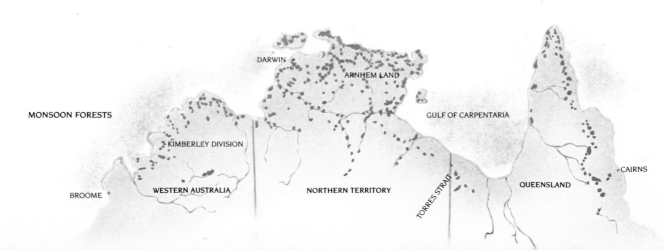

MONSOON FORESTS

DARWIN

ARNHEM LAND

GULF OF CARPENTARIA

KIMBERLEY DIVISION

BROOME

WESTERN AUSTRALIA

NORTHERN TERRITORY

TORRES STRAIT

QUEENSLAND

CAIRNS

A number of plants do not demonstrate this nomadic character, however, and occur in isolated, widely separated communities, sometimes 1000 kilometres apart, on spring habitats which apparently remained viable over the long drought of the ice ages. For example, *Elaeocarpus grandis* and *Horsfieldia australiana* grow on Cape York and also in the Top End of the Northern Territory. Fragmented distribution is also exhibited by species that are unable to spread their seeds much beyond their own canopies. Plants such as the deep green *Allosyncarpia ternata* and the *Xanthostemon* species, named after their golden masses of stamens, bear dry seeds which are relatively unattractive to birds and which simply fall to the ground.

LOCATION

Monsoon rainforest or vine forest patches occur in three main regions: the Kimberleys in small and very depauperate stands; on the Top End of the Northern Territory within the area that receives 500 millimetres annual rainfall; and on Cape York Peninsula. The area of these forest patches varies from 0.2 hectare to 500 hectares. By far the greater proportion of patches as well as the most diverse and complex vegetation, lies along a narrow coastal and subcoastal belt. They become increasingly scattered inland and ultimately are confined to very specialised refuges such as Mataranka Springs and the limestone dolines south of Katherine. Six habitat types are utilised by monsoon forest:

COASTAL LANDFORMS: hind dunes, old beach ridges and swales of retreating coasts, islands of laterite within mangroves, and headland features where year-round water is available.

LOWLAND SPRINGS AND SEEPAGE AREAS: some of these are mentioned later.

SEASONAL COASTAL AND SUBCOASTAL HABITATS: levee banks of tidal rivers and where laterite is covered by water-washed sand, where lateritic undulations dip under floodplain sediments or meet the sea, or where deposits of sand sit over clays.

SANDSTONE SPRINGS: where scarps and gullies retreat exposing underlying finer sediments which are relatively impervious.

SEASONALLY DRY ESCARPMENT: gullies and sandstone scree with protected southern aspects. The tree *Allosyncarpia* appears to be as critical as the landform here, providing shelter for floor and shrub species.

ROCK OUTCROPS: deeply shattered and jointed blocks as found in dolerite, limestone and granite country.

Some of the most accessible places to begin to study monsoon forests are the lowland spring areas near Darwin (Howard Springs,

Seed capsules of a native hibiscus.

Berry Springs) and in the Kakadu National Park area. The Kimberleys of Western Australia appear to carry only very depauperate communities in narrow gorges and ocean-'drowned' river valleys; like far flung islands out to sea, the further the island-forest is from the main source of species, the more depauperate the species list will be. What exists there comprises a few survivors, but most have been recruited from sea and bird dispersals recently.

FOREST STRUCTURE

In 1845 Ludwig Leichhardt saw undamaged monsoon forests a few years before buffaloes and pigs began to dismember them. Even as late as 1886, Captain Carrington could write the following of the Alligator Rivers region: 'The jungle is a dense mass of luxurious tropical vegetation, consisting of large trees, all or nearly all strange to me, with a dense undergrowth, the whole interlaced with many kinds of creeper. Palms are conspicuous and orchids plentiful . . .'

A flock of magpie geese (*Anseranas semipalmata*).

Until the 1970s, little was known about the structure of monsoon forests over their range, and it was only the stimulation given by the Ranger Uranium Environmental Inquiry that promoted the deeper study of these areas. The latest study, and by far the most intensive, by Jeremy Russell-Smith for the Australian National Parks and Wildlife Service, has further highlighted our recent ignorance. The writer is greatly indebted to Russell-Smith's research.

A good place to commence a look at the structure of monsoon vine forests is Field Island, part of Kakadu National Park, in Van Diemen Gulf. The island affords a rare opportunity as the sea has protected its flora from the depredations of feral pigs and buffalo.

Landing on Field Island is practicable only at high tide. Very complex mangrove forests, carrying some 19 species, almost surround the island. At the end of an almost totally hidden beach is the site of a Maccassan trepang fishing camp, with its tell-tale well and introduced tamarind tree. Behind this beach are parallel lines of old shorelines; and on the damp areas where sand overrides laterite and clay, long deep-green hummocks of seasonally dry vine forest (a monsoon forest) lend the island a banded appearance. The bright green, dark green and grey-green mangrove bands are followed by a white sandy gap, then deep green monsoon forest, pale sand again, then olive-green eucalypt strip with elongated yellow-green swamp surrounding a red laterite-bottomed lagoon, yet more eucalypts and another monsoon forest band edging a tall grey-green paperbark forest and then a tall open forest of northern bloodwood and Darwin stringybark.

Large palm fronds shadow the forest floor leaf-litter.

Usually the edge of this monsoon forest type is protected by masses of vines, many of which bear yams, a staple food of the Aboriginal people. There, also, are the spectacular crimson and black poisonous seeds of the crab's eyes (*Abrus*) fixed to bursting pods on a vine scrambling through acacias and pale pink *Hibiscus zonatus*. Once one has negotiated this tangle, it is well to keep clear of the bright green clumps of skin-ripping leaf fans of the screw palm (*Pandanus spiralis*). Inside the barriers, no longer is the heat stifling, and deep shade creates a cool twilight. Still, the mosquitoes and persistent green ants try hard to souvenir some part of a human. In September at the height of the dry season, the great red-flowering kapok trees, *Terminalia*, Leichhardt tree and the *Gyrocarpus* which form and break through the canopy, lose their leaves and the Carpentaria palms rattle in the south-east wind. At such times the banyan, tuckeroo (*Cupaniopsis anarcardioides*) and *Maranthes* will be the remaining cool shelter for the flying-foxes.

These forests or thickets comprise plants whose fruits or seeds are water borne or bird carried, particularly by the fruit pigeons. These patches also tend to be single storeyed with a few emergents, which frequently get wiped off when a cyclone comes too near. Most of the tree species are at least partially deciduous — an adaptation to the dry season drought, and also probably the reason for the deficiency of ferns and epiphytes. However, these forests carry more flowering species than any other monsoon forest: 199 out of a total census of 327 in the Kakadu region.

Immediately behind the presently active beach on the island is a very young forest of less than a hectare which is actively accumulating species. The heart of this patch is just one huge spreading evergreen tree, *Maranthes corymbosa*, along with a single *Carpentaria acuminata* palm. A host of dependent 'lesser species' crowd in underneath, building a cell of shaded humidity. So long as a wandering cyclone doesn't flatten it or a vagrant fire eat into its edge, then perhaps another 50 years will see a healthy mature vine forest patch. This is worth recording, because, as previously stated, Field Island is one of those very rare places where neither feral pigs nor water buffaloes are present. Almost all of the lowland monsoon rainforests in the Top End of Australia are deteriorating because of these agencies and changes in the fire regime.

Seasonally dry subcoastal habitats, lowland rock outcrops and lowland spring patches are receiving the greatest battering from the feral animals, cattle and fire. Fire is an increasing threat as feral

These tangled and knotted vines in Kakadu National Park are very characteristic of monsoon forests.

The matted roots of a fig tree tightly embrace a large boulder.

Islands of living and dead monsoon rainforest trees provide perches for countless waterbirds.

Sunlight is filtered into countless shades of green by the canopy mosaic.

animals produce a more effective fire environment by creating openings, which allow entry of woody weeds and grasses. Even though healthy communities in these habitats carry some 15–20 per cent fewer species than those of the coast, they are structurally very similar.

From the lookout at Ubirr, Kakadu, a very beautiful monsoon forest occurs as a gallery forest on a creek running out of the East Alligator River. Tall (25 metres) sparse trees of kapok, dark pyramidal *Terminalia*, fresh green hummocky milkwoods, solid Leichhardt trees, a row of creamy-barked paperbarks, deep-green cluster figs and shining crowns of *Livistona benthamii* stand up out of Cahills Plain, Nadab of the Aboriginal people. Crowding around the edges of the tall trees, locking in the humidity, are *Ficus scobina*, *Hibiscus* species and the screw palm. Delightful as it looks, all is not well there. These extremely important genetic corridors, where the forest lies along river levees, like the rest of the lowland forests have been seriously damaged by the grazing and wallowing of the ungulates. The structure of the forest floor is grossly altered, to such an extent that beyond Cannon Hill to the north almost every tree has collapsed into the billabong.

The types of monsoon forest in northern Australia grade from one to another, and this is clearly seen with the sandstone spring types. Complex evergreen monsoon forests developed in dissected sandstone landscapes are significantly protected from damage by stock and fire. Superb examples of this type lie in Boralba Creek and Radon Springs in Kakadu.

The forest is approached via the parched open valley. As the valley walls draw nearer, deep sandy soils cover the floor, with paperbarks, pandanus palms, grevilleas, ghost gums and *Allosyncarpia ternata*, the tree that Leichhardt described as a 'rough barked box', becoming more dense along the creek. Then out of the bright heat one enters a canopy 20–35 metres above, mainly of the deep green *Allosyncarpia* and on into the cooler, heavily humid green world. Outside the air is dry and spicy, inside heavy with the smell of rotting litter and wet earth. Deeper into the forest a number of species, some buttressed, vie for dominance with *Allosyncarpia* — *Buchanania arborescens*, *Calophyllum sil*, Carpentaria palms and a couple of white apple species. A tangle of surface roots, ferns, sedges and sand dam and divert the clear-running stream. Just a few slender lianes loop down from the canopy. On the drier verges amid the tallus lawyer vine, *Smilax australis*, *Abrus* and dense mats of the reed-cane vine (*Flagellaria indica*) tie in the edge species. Rock-wall seepages carry numerous mosses, and some 26 species of fern grow in these places and on dry rock faces. On rare occasions, floods following cyclonic

The sparser foliage of monsoonal forests reflects more light than most rainforests.

rains carry away whole patches of such forest. Here the patches range in size from pockets less than 0.1 hectare to very rare and extensive riparian areas 10 kilometres long and 50 metres wide as on Melville Island and the Arnhem Land escarpment valleys.

From the air, monsoon forest patches are seen as remarkably contrasting patches of deep green which fill the breaks in the sandstone escarpment and appear, in places, on the Arnhem Land plateau. Their classification ranges from Simple Semi-evergreen Vine Forest to Semi-deciduous Vine Forest, the degree of deciduosity being related to the length of the seasonal drought. In the semi-evergreen type, the critical plant is *Allosyncarpia ternata*, which provides the protective crown forming almost the total canopy. The semi-deciduous type comprises almost the same undercanopy species, but the canopy is supplied by another sclerophyllous tree such as *Xanthostemon psidioides*.

The importance of these escarpment patches can be seen from the fact that there are 10 more species recorded there than there are for the sandstone spring communities — further evidence that, as plant communities, the monsoon forests are well adapted to drought. Rigorous climatic sifting has eliminated the less able. The question that must be asked is whether European settlement and its activities have increased pressure on plant communities and set in train another wave of local and regional extinctions.

Agile wallabies (*Macropus agilis*) graze on floodplains beside a wall of monsoon forest.

WILDLIFE

It is not surprising that monsoon forests, which have undergone such environmental stress and most communities of which are so dispersed and far separated from the major areas of Australian rainforest, are depauperate in vertebrate fauna. Of the mammals, only three species are regular users of these Top End vine-forest habitats. The grassland melomys, a small khaki-coloured rat, lives in the grassy verge of the forest foraging in and out of the edge. The rock ringtail possum shares the broken and fissured escarpments of Arnhem Land and the Kimberleys with vine-forest species, nocturnally feeding on the blossoms and fruit of *Terminalia* and *Vitex glabrata*. Probably the only truly monsoon forest mammalian inhabitant west of Cape York is the large rock-rat, which depends on fruits especially in the late dry/early wet seasons. Other species which have been observed are the brush-tailed rabbit-rat which utilises monsoon forest in both the Kimberleys and Arnhem Land, and the northern quoll which hunts into the vine forests, although prey is not common there.

Cape York monsoon forests, however, because they are contiguous with or accessible from the main rainforest regions, do contain the richest of the monsoon forest fauna. Three of these are the white-tailed rat, prehensile-tailed rat and the rare Cape York melomys. North of Iron Range lives the only endemic mammal of the Cape, the appealing, nocturnal marsupial mouse named the cinnamon antechinus, about which little is known other than that it is a voracious eater of invertebrates and lives in tree hollows. The common ringtail possum, though rare in this area, probably makes use of conveniently placed monsoon forest. Other marsupials that may be found in these areas and the vine forest fringes are the striped possum, the spotted and the grey cuscus, the feathertail glider and the red-legged pademelon.

At least six bats have special requirements of the vine forests. The black flying-fox and the little red flying-fox frequently camp in the tall trees of the forest and obtain much of their fruit food there, while the spectacled flying-fox feeds on Cape York vine forest fruits. Three small bats, the Timor pipistrelle, the hoary bat and the Arnhem Land long-eared bat, regularly hunt flying invertebrates over and within the canopy.

Perhaps the most significant wildlife elements for the Kimberleys and the Top End are the fruit pigeons, which have been responsible for the long-distance transport of many monsoon forest fruiting species. Of particular importance are the Torresian imperial pigeon (or Torres Strait pigeon) and, to a lesser extent, the rose-crowned fruit-dove (or red-crowned pigeon), which move seed from east to west in their annual movement following the fruiting seasons. This continual enrichment of the communities from the east has been critical for revitalising the monsoon forests following short-term disasters, long-term climatic deterioration, coastal and subcoastal landform evolution, fire, and now feral animals. There is a drift the other way as the birds return east, but this is not so important to the forests of Cape York Peninsula because they are contiguous with the rainforests of the east.

While the bird lists of species using the monsoon forests are quite extensive – particularly the species that use these forests as a refuge from the late dry season – two other groups are worth mentioning and are tied to the vine forests and thickets. Firstly, the iridescent 'opals' of birds, the pittas, which forage in the litter: the noisy pitta and the red-bellied pitta occur in Cape York Peninsula; the most beautiful, the rainbow pitta, inhabits the Kimberley and Top End forests. The other is a mound builder, the scrub fowl. Old mounds built long ago by the scrub fowl have been most useful in

An Australian pelican (*Pelecanus conspicillatus*) glides upon a monsoonal lagoon.

Paperbark trees are a characteristic component of monsoon forests.

determining the past patterns of monsoon forest distribution (they have even been carbon dated) and show a rapid recent reduction in these plant communities.

Only one other vertebrate, a microhylid frog, *Sphenophyrne robusta*, is considered by the most recent studies of the monsoon forests of Kakadu to be a regular user of those habitats. The Cape York forests we would expect to be significantly richer in reptile species, yet like the birds and invertebrates, many reptiles use vine forests and thickets apparently only as refuges when the dry season peaks. The colourful little skink (*Carlia* sp.) is frequently seen in the litter of the floor.

Little is known about the invertebrates except that in 1980 one collection gathered 4500 arachnids and 5500 insect species from a number of escarpment and lowland monsoon forest habitats of Kakadu. Until much more wildlife and ecological research is done on the monsoon forests, no one can be certain what is there, how the system works or how to effectively manage them.

HISTORY OF HUMAN USE

Most of the monsoon vine forest patches in the Kimberleys are inaccessible, and apart from inland spring and streamside patches, they stay unaffected by present-day use except for the impact of changed fire and hunting regimes of the Aboriginal people. However, vine forest species on streams taken up by pastoralists have suffered from trampling, opening of the structure, drying of the environment and the subsequent destruction by wildfire.

Five attempts were made to settle the Top End before successful establishment took place at Palmerston, now Darwin. Miners, pastoralists and dreamers began their optimistic lives, most ending in despair. Water in the dry season was the paramount resource, so most accessible springs were soon either locked into the homestead settlements or into cattle management with inevitable damage to their ecosystems. In the meantime banteng cattle, which remained on Cobourg Peninsula, and the water buffalo began their rampage. Released by the first unsuccessful settlers at Raffles Bay, Cobourg Peninsula, in 1829, buffaloes soon became established. By 1845 Leichhardt found them in herds 100 kilometres away, and by the 1860s they had crossed the East Alligator River. The astute Captain Carrington in 1886, while surveying for farm lands on the Alligator River floodplains, wrote that the buffaloes were increasing rapidly, '... and if some preventative measures are not taken it is only a question of time when they will so increase as to become a serious evil.'

It was only a question of time. But the opportunist Europeans

Pandanus (*left*) and paperbark (*right*) trees line the vegetated surface of a creek.

found that at least buffaloes were successful and could carry a hide industry. Hence the buffalo shooters arrived and brought with them alcohol, disease and prostitution. The devastating pollution of the Aboriginal culture began in earnest and with it the diminution of the authority of tradition. Traditional land management with its time-tried use of fire, hunting, movements, and environmental relationships changed. The monsoon forest patches which had adapted not only to climate, soils and water, but also to the long-maintained Aboriginal traditions, thus had major changes taking place in their environment, perhaps the most critical of which was the change in the fire regime.

So buffaloes directly and indirectly caused major environmental changes. They pounded down the soil, tore through surface root nets, cut swim channels from freshwater lagoons and swamps to salt water causing the salting of major freshwater areas. By developing wallows in the shade of monsoon forest trees on streamside banks they caused them to collapse. They physically damaged thickets and forest patches by breaking down the edges and drying out the atmosphere and soil, and used the thickets and forest patches as refuges and retreats. They also radically altered the nutrient status of seepage and spring waters through their habit of storing body wastes until they could defecate in wallows and water. The effect of these changes in the environment of the monsoon forest patches was to reduce their density, dry them out, introduce woody weeds and grasses, generally to prepare them for fire. Indirectly, by causing a shift in Aboriginal cultural and traditional behaviour, the finely adapted firing regimes of the Aboriginal people broke down, leading to catastrophic fires in the late dry season which burned deeply into the patches.

On the pastoral leases, cattle tended to act in the same way. Fortunately no serious timber industry attacked the monsoon forests of the Top End. It is interesting to note that Chinese timbergetters almost cleaned out the cypress pine, much of which grew near monsoon forest areas. They completely cleaned off Barron Island (near Field Island), which has now become mainly monsoon forest.

The effect of the pastoral industry on Cape York Peninsula forests was similar to that already described. Prior to the recent period of greater environmental awareness, the only safe monsoon forest lay in the inaccessible gorges and escarpments and on offshore islands. But as a plant community it has passed through many past environmental crises . . . it is very resilient and, short of physical destruction, perhaps will survive if we let it.

Remarkable stilt roots provide additional footing for trees in monsoonal forests on rocky substrate.

In Kakadu National Park monsoonal rainforest flourishes in the shelter of rock escarpments and gorges.

The following statement on the conservation of the monsoon forest was produced by Jeremy Russell-Smith of the Australian National University and by Clyde Dunlop, botantist with the Conservation Commission of the Northern Territory, after an exhaustive study (1984). Minor alterations have been made by the author.

'Land tenure in the Northern Territory's Top End falls into three main categories: leasehold (mainly grazing leases), Aboriginal land and National Parks and reserves. The amount of land held under freehold title is quite minor and will not be considered here. The point must be made that land tenure is changing rapidly at the present time. Much of the land mapped as leasehold is under Aboriginal land claim and so in future may be Aboriginal land. There is also an Aboriginal land claim on the Katherine Gorge National Park and on some small conservation reserves held by the Conservation Commission of the Northern Territory. Kakadu National Park is also expanding and will in the near future encompass the two leasehold blocks on its southern boundary and thus will virtually abut the borders of Katherine Gorge National Park.

'Kakadu National Park and Cobourg National Park are in fact under Aboriginal ownership; Kakadu has been leased by Australian National Parks and Wildlife Service, and Cobourg is jointly managed by the traditional Aboriginal owners and the Conservation Commission of the Northern Territory.

'It is clear that the largest tracts of land are either leasehold or under Aboriginal ownership. Aboriginal land for the most part is not intensively developed for agriculture or pastoral pursuits and so must be regarded as affording a reasonable level of protection for the monsoon vine-forests.

Magpie geese forage by 'up-ending' in shallow monsoonal wetlands.

'On the basis of the six habitat types, the best conserved are the dry sandstone and sandstone spring forests. These are well represented in Arnhem Land, Kakadu National Park and Melville Island. There are also good, well-protected representatives of this type under private ownership on the Mt Tolmer escarpment south-west of Darwin. The coastal, subcoastal and lowland spring habitats are reasonably well represented in reserves, though a couple of outstanding examples of lowland spring forest in the Darwin–Daly region are in urgent need of effective conservation management. On the other hand, very few of the rock outcrop habitats and the hinterland *Acacia shirleyi*-type thickets enjoy legal protection, though many of these situations are to a large degree protected topographically.

'For the future acquisition of monsoon vine-forest for conserva-

The estuarine or saltwater crocodile (*Crocodylus porosus*) frequents lowland and monsoonal rainforest.

A typical paperbark- and pandanus-dominated monsoon rainforest fringing a lily lagoon.

Water lilies thrive in the warm shallow lagoon waters and attract numerous pollinating insects.

Monsoonal vine forest and creek bed in dry season.

tion purposes, attention is drawn to the necessity for appreciating that patches and populations do not necessarily exist in isolation. The long-term viability of these patches may well be dependent on conserving the diffuse genetic connections between them (e.g., riparian habitats). For rational assessment of future conservation requirements, an ecological survey of inland vine-forests is urgently needed.

A narrow creek exposes the rock substrate of this monsoon forest.

'While much vine-forest habitat is already, or likely to be protected by forms of land tenure which are conducive for conservation, the small sizes of most patches means that they are vulnerable to certain types of continued disturbance. For the most part, vine-forests in the Northern Territory have been little affected by the direct impact of European settlement. In contrast to eastern Australia, such clearance of 'jungle' patches, and logging, which has occurred, has been both highly localised and relatively insignificant. It is improbable that such activities have affected the status of any taxon, plant or animal. The most serious threat to the integrity of patches concerns their utilisation by feral and domestic ungulates especially the introduced water buffalo, and through the rooting up of regeneration by pigs. With respect to ungulates, such utilisation leads to the creation of both woody fuels (though habitat destruction) and fine fuels (through promoting the spread of native and exotic weedy species). Such a situation, in combination with the widespread practice of frequent late-dry-season burning, can lead to rapid retreat of patch boundaries. While uncontrolled feral and domestic ungulate numbers are likely to be greatly reduced under Government policy aimed at eradicating brucellosis and tuberculosis by 1992, it is questionable whether this will significantly release pressure from monsoon vine-forests in many situations. Such pessimism is based both on the geographical scale of the problem as well as the observations that: in the event of shooting or catching activities, buffalo often seek refuge in vine-forest habitats; and even small numbers of animals can occasion severe damage, especially in fragile spring habitats. Thus, despite the relative degree of legislated protection which monsoon vine-forests in the Northern Territory enjoy, many threatened and significant patches are presently, and for the foreseeable future, beyond the means of effective conservation.

'Outside urban areas, exotic weeds are not a serious problem at the present time. While *Hyptis suaveolens* and *Passiflora foetida* are now so widespread as to be considered naturalised, only one species, *Lantana camara*, currently restricted to the Darwin region, presents a potential threat given its highly aggressive habit. More ominous, especially to vine-forest invertebrates, is the recent arrival of the cane toad (*Bufo marinus*) at the Queensland–Northern Territory border.'

So far as the Kimberley area is concerned, the vast Prince Regent River Flora and Fauna Reserve, the Drysdale River National Park and the Aboriginal Reserves (pending the new Land Rights Act) should secure the small areas of monsoon forests there.

The Queensland situation is always unique. There seems to be little attention given to conservation priorities in many of their reserve establishments. Queensland requires the kind of comprehensive investigation of conservation needs that occurred in Western Australia and the Northern Territory. As the homeland of rainforest species, Queensland's role in the preservation of rainforest is critical... and preservation must mean management as well as adequate reservation.

Spotted cuscus (Phalanger maculatus)

4

SUBTROPICAL RAINFORESTS

DAVID ALLWORTH

IN THE TIMES before Australia separated from Antarctica, and the ice-caps formed, seasonally mild rainforest covered much of the land. Many scientists believe that the subtropical rainforests of today most closely resemble a major part of those ancient forests; and these subtropical forests are the ancestral home of many of Australia's modern plant and animal species. The separation of Australia and Antarctica signalled the end of the great southern continent, Gondwanaland, and the contraction of those extensive ancient rainforests.

Today, subtropical rainforest is found from the lowlands of the south coast of New South Wales to the uplands of northern Queensland. The main occurrence of subtropical rainforest is from the Mackay hinterland to the mid north coast of New South Wales. A distinctive range of plant species is found throughout the subtropical rainforests of this region.

At the time of James Cook's exploration in 1770, the largest area of subtropical rainforest was centred on the New South Wales–Queensland border area. Despite the loss of the 'Big Scrub' in the Richmond River lowlands of northern New South Wales, this remains the stronghold of subtropical rainforest in Australia. However, as in other areas the forest is now confined to the foothills and mountains.

The luxuriance of the subtropical rainforest was often commented upon by the early explorers and travellers. New South Wales surveyor, Clement Hodgkinson, in the late 1830s stated: 'It grows on

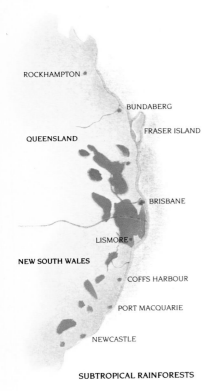

the richest alluvial land and consists of trees of almost endless variety and very large dimensions, totally differing from the ordinary Eucalypti and Casuarinae, which grow in the common open forest of Australia, for the brush trees in general possess a rich umbrageous foliage of brightshining green ... But the peculiar appearance of the brush is principally caused by the countless species of creepers, wild vines and parasitical plants of singular formation.'

To the layperson subtropical rainforests look much like the rich tropical rainforests of northern Queensland. In fact until recent times, scientific texts did not differentiate between the two. However, subtropical forests are now widely recognised as a separate subgrouping. A principal difference, according to rainforest ecologist, Dr George Baur, is that in contrast to tropical rainforest where high species diversity makes it difficult to identify a dominant species, subtropical rainforests have a tendency to be dominated by a few species. Tree species that are good indicators of subtropical rainforests are white beech, (*Gimelina leichhardtii*), booyong (*Argyrodendron* species), flame tree (*Brachychiton acerifolius*), yellow carabeen (*Sloanea woollsii*) and rose mahogany (*Dysoxylum fraserianum*).

Generally speaking, the forest is characterised by a three-layered structure. Towards the edges, giant eucalypts and brush box often tower above the closed canopy, which is usually somewhat lower than its tropical counterpart. Compared with many tropical forest structures, the understorey tends to be thicker with denser shrubs, although this varies with many other factors.

While not as rich in plant species as the tropical forests, the subtropical rainforests still contain a profusion of species, giving an impression of extravagant life. These forests shelter an abundance of vines, buttressed trunks, palms and epiphytes, typical of the popular image of rainforest, but there are fewer epiphytes including orchids than in the forests of the north.

The soil preference of this forest type is for rich soils of alluvial or basalt origin — red earth remnants of a major ring of volcanoes from the earth's Tertiary era. Dramatic soil changes between adjacent areas mean equally dramatic changes in the vegetation, even when rainfall and altitude are similar.

Unfortunately, the combined assets of rich red earth and adequate rainfall have meant that subtropical rainforest, particularly on accessible lowlands, has been a prime candidate for clearing and exploitation. Recent estimates have put the total area of subtropical rainforest at only 600 000 hectares over its north–south range of some 2300 kilometres.

The subtropical rainforest is the home of many rare and bizarre

The dense shrub layer underlying this subtropical rainforest includes the large-leaved cunjevoi.

A rainforest-dwelling swift moth sips flower nectar.

forms of life, perhaps none more so than the platypus frog (*Rheobatrachus silus*) which hatches its young from fertilised eggs in its stomach. Some of the world's most primitive flowering plants still inhabit the forest. The mystery of the origins of the flowering plants is yet not solved – but the subtropical rainforests, in conjunction with the tropical rainforests of north-east Queensland, are important sites for studies attempting to unravel the mystery.

On the origin of subtropical rainforest itself, one long-held view is that it is the poor cousin of the tropical rainforests in north-east Queensland, and that both these types are the result of plants invading from the Indo-Malesian region to the north. This view followed the thinking of J.D. Hooker in his *Introductory Essay to the Flora of Tasmania* (1860) and held sway for over a century. Then with the acceptance of Wegener's theory of continental drift, with its implications for climatic changes and species distribution, the thinking changed. Evidence now suggests that many of the plants and animals of Australia's rainforests are as much Australian in origin as the eucalypts and acacias. There have been invasions, particularly in recent times, but not whole forests of plants as previously thought.

The view that subtropical rainforests are the 'poor cousin' of tropical rainforests in north-east Queensland has been further refuted by rainforest ecologists Dr Len Webb and Mr J.G. Tracey. Fossil evidence shows that subtropical rainforests once existed over wide areas of the Australian continent, but with the onset of more arid times, subtropical rainforest areas became separated by dry 'corridors'. North-east Queensland rainforests became separated from rainforests in southern Queensland and northern New South Wales by dry corridors in central Queensland. The separation has existed for a long time. This is borne out by the fact that while many plant genera are shared between the two regions, numerous species of those genera are not. So the southern forests are not the result of an invasion of plants from the north (the 'poor cousin' theory), but rather they are long-separated groups of plants which have evolved independently.

Throughout the rigours of past climatic changes, subtropical rainforest has been able to exist continuously in favourable locations. The Great Dividing Range, the coastal ranges and the coastal lowlands, all with the necessary high rainfall and fertile soils, have provided an environmental refuge for the rainforests. A rich collection of animals and plant species of Gondwanan times has been able to survive in these refuge areas, being joined by many new species that evolved or invaded. It is this variety of life that is of so much interest, for its beauty and antiquity.

The red-eyed tree frog (*Litoria chloris*) is one of many subtropical forest tree frogs.

Pages 110-111. Rainforests produce and retain moisture, greatly influencing local climate.

Although a tiny fraction of this vast continent, rainforests have been estimated to contain up to 50 per cent of all plant species in Australia. The subtropical rainforest is second only to the tropical rainforest in terms of plant species richness. Many of these species are of international scientific interest.

The greatest concentration of primitive flowering plant families in the world is in the rainforests of eastern Australia. They are recognised by having reproductive structures similar to fossil records of up to 100 million years ago, when it is thought that flowering plants first started to evolve. Many occur in the uplands, which are related to the subtropical rainforests of the south. Six families of truly primitive flowering plants can be found in the subtropical rainforests. Bolwarra (*Eupomatia laurina*), one species of primitive flowering plant, is commonly found in the subtropical rainforests. Other examples of primitive flowering plants are the genera *Cryptocarya*, *Endiandra*, *Litsea*, *Cinnamomum*, *Wilkea* and *Tasmannia*.

Predating the primitive flowering plants are the conifers (pine trees). The species in the subtropical rainforests or its margins are the hoop and bunya pines (*Araucaria* spp.), she-pine (*Podocarpus elatus*) and scrub cypress (*Callitris macleayana*). Species of *Araucaria*, *Podocarpus*, and *Callitris* are all found in other countries. For example, South America has species of *Araucaria* and *Podocarpus*. This international distribution supports the theory that once Australia was much closer to a number of other continents including South America.

Particular rainforest plants may occur in areas 1000 kilometres apart, without any occurrences in between. *Phyllanthus brassii* occurs in a subtropical rainforest near Gladstone, then is not found again until the rainforests north of Cairns. Such separated occurrences help give us a picture of the past distribution of particular vegetation communities. They are like the fingerprints of the thief, telling us what has gone on and who may have been present.

One of the rainforest leaf-litter dwelling *Mixophyes* barred frogs.

Rare plants of very restricted geographical range are a feature of rainforests. A survey of 561 sites throughout Australia's rainforests showed that 12 per cent of 1316 species occurred at only one site. In New South Wales there are estimated to be 110 rare and endangered rainforest plants. The rarity or restricted nature of rainforest plants has been increased by the massive losses of rainforest. Southern penda (*Xanthostemon oppostfolius*) was described in 1929 as being 'very frequent in the Noosa Shire, in parts of which it is the most common species of the scrub.' Southern penda is now listed as endangered. Another example is onionwood (*Owenia cepiodora*) which was sought

A swiftly flowing creek redistributes leaves and other nutrients through the forests.

Moonwoolba Cascades in Lamington National Park support dense and lush vegetation.

Particularly sheltered and wet corners of the forest produce luxuriant and complex growth.

by timbergetters as a substitute for the highly valued red cedar (*Toona australis*). The log was soaked in a stream to remove the characteristic onion odour and then sold as red cedar. This species was common along the Tweed and Richmond Rivers before the 1900s. Clearing and logging have now endangered the survival of the species.

Trees of awesome size can be found in the forest. Figs can attain heights of 45 metres and have diameters of several metres. These massive plants can start their life as a small seed sending a shoot down to the ground from a high branch of a host tree. Then more shoots are sent out, engulfing the host tree. Seemingly the fig strangles its host. 'Strangler fig' is the name for *Ficus watkinsiana*, although the habit of strangling is not restricted to this species. Often the host tree dies, and a hollow is left in the middle of the fig as the dead tree rots away.

Great ages are attained. One specimen of brush box (*Lophostemon confertus*) in the Terania Creek rainforest is estimated to be 1200 years old. William the Conqueror would have been landing on the shores of England when this tree was about 300 years old.

Bursting through the rich pattern of green in the summer months is the brilliant red of the flame tree (*Brachychiton acerifolius*). If you are able to find a high vantage point over the forest canopy, this tree can be seen dotted about the forest. It and the red cedar are the two deciduous trees of the subtropical rainforest.

The most dreaded trees of the rainforest are the stingers (*Dendrocnide* spp.). One light brush against the leaves can bring horrendous pain, a pain that can recur in twinges for months. The very fine hair on both sides of the leaf is the offending part. The giant stinger (*Dendrocnide excelsa*) is possibly the largest stinging plant in the world, reaching a height of 45 metres. Stingers are most prolific at the edges of the rainforest or in sites of disturbance by humans.

Edible plants can be found in the rainforest, and the Aborigines made good use of many of the plants in their diet.

The macadamia tree (*Macadamia* spp.) is now widely cultivated for its nuts which are described as being among the world's best — but very hard to crack. The nut has a very high oil content, and once it has been lit over a flame it will burn for several minutes. Macadamia trees are the only Australian rainforest plant cultivated commercially for food production. Other plants have functional uses. An attractive palm, the piccabeen (*Archontopheonix cunninghamiana*), derives its name from *pikki*, an Aboriginal word for 'vessel'. The sheath at the base of the fronds forms a carrying vessel when the ends are tied together. The piccabeen palm is a distinctive fea-

The eastern yellow robin (*Eopsaltria australis*).

This strangler fig shows that tree buttresses may attain huge proportions both in height and floor area.

ture of the subtropical rainforests, occurring widely, particularly along creeks.

With all the powers of a subpoena, the lawyer vine palm (*Calamus muelleri*) can pull you up. On its stems are sharp hook-shaped thorns, which easily take hold of clothing or skin. The only way to release yourself is to reverse from its clutches. During the Terania Creek Inquiry, Justice Isaacs asked the eminent rainforest ecologist Dr Len Webb why the lawyer vine was so named. Dr Webb replied: 'I think, sir, it is because they have hooks, and when they get hold of you it's hard to be disentangled.' The lawyer vine has been used in basket weaving — the thorny hooks being shed from the vine as the plant becomes mature.

The walking-stick palm (*Linospadix monostachyas*), as its name implies, was used to make walking-sticks; the hand-hold was moulded from the bulb growing just below ground level. The palm is widespread, but never attains great heights.

In the moisture-laden environment, a multitude of smaller plants thrive. Epiphytes are prolific, and distinguish the subtropical rainforest from its neighbouring temperate rainforests. Epiphytes include orchids, fungi, staghorns and elkhorns, to name but a few. They live by acquiring nutrients from the air, water and falling vegetation, so they are therefore not parasites on their host plant. Entire tree-trunks can be covered by the epiphyte *Pothos longipes*, recognised by its simple narrow leaf with a pinched-in 'waist'. Elkhorns, staghorns and orchids abound at all levels of the forest.

Lianas (vines) reach enormous sizes. Pepper vines (*Piper* spp.) not only attain lengths far greater than the heights of the host tree but can be up to 20 centimetres thick in diameter. Climbing high into the canopy of the forest, they provide the classic Tarzan's vine.

The plants described here are important elements in the subtropical rainforests of Australia but are a tiny percentage of the total number of species. The subtropical rainforests, although not as species-diverse as the tropical rainforests, are still exceptionally rich, containing many plant species not found in the north Queensland forests.

FAUNA

As the sun begins to rise, the flying-foxes (*Pteropus* spp.) come home to rest, and the forest becomes a choirstall for a multitude of birds. If you remain still, the noisy pitta may pass you by. High up, a pigeon will roost. The deep guttural sound of the wompoo pigeon rings out, or the human baby cry of the catbird. Then a thump and a rustle of leaves: a small marsupial speeds by, unidentifiable as it races out of

A nestling bird awaits a parent's return.

Woody vines and lawyer vine, or *Calamus*.

Fallen leaves and flower petals enter the rainforest nutrient cycle.

The sculptured buttress of a fig tree.

Pages 122-23. Crow's nest ferns (*top*), tree ferns (*right*) and mosses (*bottom left*).

A lace monitor (*Varanus varius*).

Morning mist, tree ferns, bird's nest ferns and hanging lianes.

An adult greengrocer cicada (*Cyclochila australasine*) emerges from its nymphal skin.

sight. If you sift through the leaf litter that lies on the red earth, you will find small forms of life busy carrying out the processes of breaking down organic matter.

The subtropical rainforest is typified by a large number of animals that move between it and the adjacent sclerophyll forest areas. Similarly, the mammal, bird, reptile and insect species can be found in both the moist eucalypt forest and the rainforest. This contrasts with the tropical rainforests where very clear groups of mammals, birds, reptiles, etc., are confined to the rainforest habitat. In the tropical rainforest you are also likely to find birds restricted to either highlands or lowlands; but such a distinction loses its sharpness in the subtropical areas.

Like many of the plants, the animals of the rainforest exhibit very clear relationships with the animal life that existed in Gondwanan times. This is understandable, because throughout the rigours of climatic change from the late Tertiary era to the present, rainforest has always existed in locations that provided a suitable habitat for these animals to survive.

Amongst the most mysterious of animals is the platypus frog, (*Rheobatrachus silus*). Found in 1973 in the Sunshine Coast hinterland, this rather plain frog has an extraordinary life pattern: it swallows its fertilised eggs into its stomach, which then becomes a womb, from which fully formed frogs (rather than tadpoles) are hatched. The young arrive into the world through the parent's mouth. The frog appears to have the capacity to instantly switch off the digestive capacity of its stomach, and this aspect has been the subject of extensive study by scientists for its potential application to the treatment of gastric ulcers in humans. Found in the still pools of mountain streams, this frog was relatively widespread when first discovered. However, since then there have been many dry seasons, and it has not been seen for several years. Some people fear extinction, although a similar species has recently been found in the Mackay region.

The hip pocket frog (*Assa darlingtoni*) also has unusual reproductive habits. The eggs are laid by the female, fertilised by the male and transferred to the brood pouches in the male's flanks. Frogs of all kinds are easily heard in the rainforest on a damp summer's evening. They comprise one half of the forest duo: the other half is the birds.

Many birds of the subtropical rainforest are also found in the tropical rainforests – the wompoo pigeon, noisy pitta and satin bowerbird, for example. There are others, however, that are entirely

A giant fig supports a host of climbing and epiphytic plants.

restricted to subtropical rainforests — regent bowerbird, Albert's lyrebird and wonga pigeon. The birds occupy various strata in the rainforest. On the forest floor the noisy pitta, regent bowerbird, and eastern yellow robin move about in search of insects, while the wompoo pigeon, king parrot, and Lewin's honeyeater are more likely to be in the canopy feeding on fruits.

Albert's lyrebird (*Menura alberti*) differs from its cousin, the superb lyrebird, in lacking the famous flamboyant tail. It is rarely seen but makes resonant calls and mimics other birds. At mating time, the male chooses a log or a clearing as a display arena. Lyrebirds are members of the family Menuridae, one of the twelve families of birds thought to have inhabited this continent since the breakup of Gondwanaland.

Desiring all things blue is the satin bowerbird. The male of the species, known for its brilliant black-blue sheen and startling china-blue eyes, prepares a bower for the mating season which is decorated with any blue item available. A simple structure of twigs and sticks, the bower has two parallel walls and is made on the ground. In one bower an observer counted 34 pieces of blue glass, 10 pieces of blue matchboxes, eight blue bags, four blue chocolate papers, and one blue envelope, to name only a few of the items present.

The call of the catbird, a plaintive 'meeow', is commonly heard in the early morning or at dusk. Feeding on native fruits and berries, the catbird resides high in the trees, from where its mournful wail can be heard but its exquisite emerald-green plumage seldom observed.

One of the many beautiful *Sarcochilus* rainforest orchids.

More easily observed is the scrub turkey (*Alectura lathami*) which is found in both subtropical and tropical rainforests. Its conspicuous mound can be over a metre high and several metres across. In this mound the eggs are laid and their incubation is entirely dependent on the fermentation of the mound. The right temperature is required to incubate the eggs. The male of the species ensures this by raking about on the mound with powerful legs, either removing or building up parts of the mound to control temperature. Although the scrub turkey is a ground-dwelling bird, it will fly in order to escape from danger.

A number of very rare birds inhabit the rainforest, among them the rufous scrub-bird and Coxen's fig parrot. The extent and diversity of rainforest is very important to the fruit-eating birds. Because trees bear fruits at only particular times of the year, those birds requiring a year-round supply need many tree species over a wide geographical range to ensure continuity in the supply of the fruit. In a particular region it is also important to retain rainforest in both the lowlands and uplands, because it has been observed that trees of the

Tree ferns and other ferns.

The red-necked pademelon.

Sparring red-necked pademelons (*Thylogale thetis*).

Pages 132- 33. Stinging shrubs (*Dendrocnide* sp.), (*right*), prefer track-edge or disturbed rainforest.

same species may fruit up to four weeks earlier in the lowlands of the region than in the uplands. This staggering of fruiting times is integral to a continuous food supply.

When the noise of the birds at dawn ceases for a moment, the rustle of leaves may be heard as a mammal passes by. On the edges of the rainforest the pademelon grazes on grasses and green leaves. Its well-made tracks are purposely followed as sustenance is sought. Pademelons are small wallabies with a dash of red on either the shoulder or leg, depending on the species. They are commonly seen and can become quite tame if left in peace.

The long-nosed potoroo, which in 1789 was the first mammal described and drawn by the First Fleeters is now rare. This fleet-footed small marsupial is part of the Potoroidae family which retains features of the original arboreal possum-like stock from which the kangaroos are descended. The most primitively formed Potoroidae member is the musky rat-kangaroo (*Hypsiprymnodon moschatus*), of the tropical rainforest. The potoroo of the subtropical region appears more developed. Potoroos are now regarded as rare over most of their range.

The bobuck or mountain brushtail possum (*Trichosurus caninus*), with its cat-like ears, and the common ringtail possum (*Pseudocheirus peregrinus*), with its distinctive tightly curled tail, are commonly found in the subtropical rainforest. Both of these species find that the old gnarled emergent eucalypts of the rainforest provide a valuable home. The bobuck's distribution is generally restricted to the wet forest south of the south-east corner of Queensland. The common ringtail possum is widely dispersed, with a subspecies occurring in the rainforest at the eastern border of Queensland and New South Wales.

Native leek (*Bulbine bulbosa*).

A curiosity of the forest is a tiny marsupial, the brown antechinus (*Antechinus stuartii*), fated to death by its sexual activity. At about one year old, all males die after an intense period of mating. It appears that death is a result of stress, frequent aggressive encounters and the reduction of the effectiveness of their immune system by stress hormones.

As with the mammals, many reptiles range between the rainforest and other forest types. The red-bellied black snake and the eastern water dragon are among these. Well camouflaged in the rainforest is the southern angle-headed dragon (*Gonocephalus sinipes*). In the dappled light of the rainforest, this animal is hard to see, but once you have your eye on one of these beasts you can have a good look as it relies on camouflage rather than speed to protect itself.

Integral to the processes of the rainforest is the small life: the

A rich diversity of subtropical rainforest plant life, featuring the large-leaved cunjevois.

The spectacular adult male regent bowerbird (*Sericulus chrysocephalus*).

insects, worms, butterflies, weevils. A wasp fertilises a fig, millipedes break down the fibre of a fallen log, snails help to convert the fallen leaves into humus. Our knowledge of the smaller life is patchy — many new species are still being found, and research into their distribution and habits has hardly begun.

Among the most beautiful small creatures of the rainforest are the butterflies. Their fragile form fluttering and drifting through the shafts of light briefly illuminating their exquisite colours is part of the poetry of a walk through a rainforest. One of the most spectacular butterflies is the Richmond birdwing (*Ornithoptera richmondia*) which is found in the subtropical rainforests of the border ranges and southern Queensland. Butterflies are important pollinators of plants, thereby playing a key role in the ecology of the forests.

HISTORY OF HUMAN USE

The human history of the rainforest goes back into the legends of the indigenous inhabitants of Australia — the Aborigines. Our record of their association with the forest is incomplete, such was the haste with which they were removed when the white settlers arrived. We know that in southern Queensland two distinct groups of Aborigines existed: those of the coast, the fishing people; and those of the mountains, the rainforest dwellers. Much of the plant life played an important part in the Aboriginal lifestyle, and many features of the rainforest region's landscape have legends associated with them.

Each year the bunya pines bear seeds, but only every third or fourth year is a prolific crop produced. At these times Aboriginal tribes from the Clarence River in northern New South Wales to the Dawson River in central Queensland used to converge on the Bunya Mountains area extending from the Blackall Ranges, on the Sunshine coast, to the Bunya Mountains themselves, edging the Darling Downs. Bunya trees were regarded as sacred, and individual families had rights to particular trees. In the early days of white settlement, when one bunya tree was felled timbergetters fled the area in fear. Tom Petrie, an early settler of the Moreton region, instanced tribal warfare because a bunya tree was axed. Governor Gipps recognised the importance of bunya trees as a food source for the Aborigines, affording them complete protection in 1842. This protection lapsed in time, and bunyas became an important component of southern Queensland timber supply.

Early writings refer to a healthy and plentiful lifestyle being enjoyed by the Aborigines of coastal and rainforest regions. Sadly, this culture met catastrophe quickly and savagely. The Great Divid-

The radiating fronds of epiphytic bird's nest fern (*Asplenium nidus*) catch fallen leaves for nutrition.

Pages 138- 39. The diversity of fern species in rainforest is perhaps greatest on creek edges.

A cloud-enshrouded rainforest canopy in Lamington National Park.

Larger tree-trunks support countless forms of climbing and epiphytic plant life.

A violet stick insect (*Didymuria violescens*).

ing Range where rainforests had had refuge from the rigours of climatic change was to become the refuge for Aborigines hounded from the coastal plains and tablelands. From there a guerilla war was conducted, but the mountains could neither support them in food year-round nor protect them from the guns of the white settlers.

Accompanying this murderous assault on the indigenous people, an equally fatal attack was unleashed on the indigenous forest. Subtropical rainforest that had survived in particular locations for millions of years had no defence against the axe and the match. Cedargetters spearheaded the assault in the search for 'red gold'. At first they logged the limited rainforest along the Hawkesbury River, then moved up the coast, reaching the Richmond River by 1842. The most northerly stand of red cedar was in the tropical rainforests of the Daintree in far north Queensland, and this fell under the axe by 1873.

Following hard on the heels of the axemen were the agriculturalists, attracted by the richness of the red earths where subtropical rainforest had grown. For butter, potatoes and sugarcane – and a meagre living – the Comboyne Plateau, Dorrigo Plateau, Mt Tamborine, Maleny Plateau, 'Big Scrub', Childers, Dalrymple Heights and coastal lowland forests were razed. At the time of Captain Cook, the Big Scrub, said to be Australia's largest area of tall subtropical rainforests, was 750 square kilometres or 75 000 hectares; today, barely 300 hectares remain. Initially the cleared lands proved fertile, but fertility declined and gradually these areas were invaded by weeds and lower-quality grasses.

CONSERVATION STATUS

Clearing proceeded at such a pace that a huge number of valuable timber trees, some of Australia's finest cabinet woods, were burnt for want of an immediate market. In the 1870s a battle developed between those concerned to see areas of valuable timber reserved to produce timber in perpetuity and the agriculturalists seeking to clear more land. It was a battle that was to be widespread and bitter until after World War Two.

Only a short period after the start of this battle came the push for national parks. In 1878 Robert Collins, from Queensland, visited the United States and was inspired by the national parks ideal. Living in sight of the McPherson Range on the New South Wales–Queensland border he campaigned for their protection as national park. On 31 July 1915, two years after Collins's death and following valuable work by Romeo Lahey, a civil engineer (and son of a sawmiller), 19 000 hectares were set aside as Lamington National Park.

Subtropical rainforest understorey: saplings, vines and tree ferns.

A female satin bowerbird feeds her chicks a rainforest fruit.

A male satin bowerbird (*Ptilonorhynchus violaceus*) displays to a female crouching within his bower.

Satin bowerbird chicks beg as their mother approaches.

The brilliant red flowers of a distant flame tree, (*Brachychiton acerifolius*) in Dorrigo National Park.

This was not the first rainforest national park in Queensland. Witches Falls, at Mt Tamborine, the Bunya Mountains, and Cunningham's Gap preceded it.

In October 1903 the Inspector of Forests, G.G. Board, inspected the Bunya Mountains, and although in his annual report he referred to the large quantities of timber, he nevertheless recommended that the area be made a national park because of its special values. In 1908 the Bunya Mountains were protected.

In New South Wales Phillip Wright (later the Chancellor of the University of New England), with the assistance of Earl Page (politician, and Prime Minister in April 1939), campaigned for the establishment of the New England National Park. In central Queensland, Eungella National Park was declared after citizen pressure in the 1930s. An area of 50 000 hectares became national park, containing 30 000 hectares of rainforest. It was to be Queensland's largest rainforest park for many years.

A male king parrot
(*Alisterus scapularis*).

Today the battle for recognition of the special values of rainforests goes on in many areas. For years the National Parks Associations, the Australian Conservation Foundation, and other citizen-based groups have made representations to governments to have areas protected. Some of those representations have been heeded, but others have not.

In 1978 colourful citizens, sitting in front of bulldozers in an effort to stop the logging of the subtropical rainforests of Terania Creek, brought the case for the preservation of rainforests finally on to the TV screens of the nation. The bulldozers were halted in Terania, and an arduous, often bitter and very heated struggle between conservationists and the ailing timber industry for the protection of all New South Wales rainforests followed. In 1982, Premier Wran announced an extensive 'package' of national park reservations over the rainforests of the state. Not all rainforests were encompassed, and logging is still continuing in some today.

Analysis of the Wran decision shows that although significant areas are now protected there are still very serious gaps in the conservation of certain rare plants. Only 42 of the 110 rare plants in the subtropical and temperate rainforests of New South Wales are protected in reserves. And only half of the subtropical rainforest subtypes are adequately conserved. Further work is needed to fill the gaps.

Applying itself to the problem of alternative timber supplies and job opportunities, the New South Wales Government was able to come up with a plan to preserve extensive areas of rainforest and yet maintain the employment prospects in the timber industry. The solution was the finding that non-rainforest timbers could perform

Walking-stick palms (*foreground*), buttresses and strangler figs (*left*) in Dorrigo National Park.

Dense climbing vines typically clad rainforest edge trees.

Morans Falls, Lamington National Park.

many of the functions of rainforest timbers. For instance, it was found that eucalypt timbers could be made into plywood, and other timbers could be used for school desk tops previously made, in part, from rainforest timbers.

In Queensland the plantations of hoop pine, a rainforest tree, could immediately ease the pressure on logging natural subtropical rainforests. There are at present 420 square kilometres of hoop pine plantation in Queensland, much of it ready for felling. In the longer term an examination must be made of reforesting lands with many different rainforest species to ensure supplies of their valuable timber.

Unfortunately, in Queensland the initial pre-war gains of Eungella, the Bunyas, Cunningham's Gap and Lamington National Parks have not been augmented. Major tracts of subtropical rainforest have either very small parks or no parks at all, and areas are still being cleared for agriculture, dams and pine plantations. Logging is the most serious threat to the remaining areas in Queensland. To the west of Brisbane, parts of the Scenic Rim are being logged, as are areas west of the Sunshine Coast, in the Bundaberg hinterland, Gladstone hinterland and at Mackay.

A major obstacle to halting the logging of rainforests is employment and timber supply considerations. Alternative employment opportunities and timber supply strategies have been suggested, which involve reforesting already-cleared lands, and the substitution of existing plantation timbers for those from natural rainforest areas – similar strategies to those used in New South Wales. The New South Wales Government is preparing a submission for UNESCO to place extensive areas of the state's rainforest on the World Heritage list. Logically, the rainforests of Queensland should join this nomination and so give recognition that these forests are of international importance.

Fallen *Pandorea* flowers litter the forest floor.

Generally the conservation status of subtropical rainforest from central New South Wales to Mackay is poor. Lowland rainforest can be measured in only a few hundred hectares of what may have been an area in excess of 100 000 hectares at the time of Cook. Chances for adequate conservation have gone.

Numerous areas of undulating plateau rainforest have been completely cleared. However, a few fine examples remain in areas such as the Bunya Mountains and the McPherson Range. With few exceptions, therefore, it is the mountain tops, their slopes and gorges that are the stronghold of subtropical rainforests. In these rugged regions it is possible to make further large gains for the protection of subtropical rainforest. Many of these steep, rugged sites have already been conserved in part and are probably one of the better conserved landscapes in Australia.

Foliage of a giant stinging tree (*Dendrocnide excelsa*).

Regent bowerbird (Sericulus chrysocephalus)

5

WARM TEMPERATE RAINFORESTS

ALEX FLOYD

THE FIRST IMPRESSION of a warm temperate rainforest is one of comparative tidiness and uniformity compared with the extravagant baroque of tropical and subtropical associations. The festooned, buttressed giants of these forests are replaced with comparatively slender unbuttressed trees of a more uniform height. The even canopy usually reaches 25–30 metres and the number of tree species forming the canopy is small, often being only between three and fifteen. The most common floristic ingredient of a warm temperate rainforest is the coachwood – a beautiful, straight tree whose smooth grey bark is decoratively encrusted with pink, orange, grey and white lichens. Forests of coachwood and other smooth-barked species of uniform appearance can call to mind a planted forest. This impression of conformity is aptly described as 'simple' in Dr Len Webb's classification of this forest as Simple Notophyll Evergreen Vine Forest.

LOCATION

Warm temperate rainforest extends discontinuously from the Atherton Tableland in Queensland to East Gippsland, Victoria, on the relatively poorer soils derived from metamorphic, sedimentary and quartz-rich igneous rocks such as rhyolite and granite, where rainfall is well distributed throughout the year and generally in excess of 1300 millimetres annually. Because of its preference for cool condi-

QUEENSLAND

BRUNSWICK HEADS

Clarence R.

WASHPOOL

NEW SOUTH WALES

COFFS
HARBOUR

Macleay R.

PORT
MACQUARIE

Manning R.

BARRINGTON
TOPS

Hunter R.

NEWCASTLE

BLUE
MTNS

Hawkesbury R.

SYDNEY

Shoalhaven R.

BATEMANS BAY

**WARM TEMPERATE RAINFOREST
AREAS IN NEW SOUTH WALES**

EDEN

tions it occurs from the tablelands in the north to the coast in the south. Its best development is in New South Wales, north of the Hunter River, where there are 23 500 hectares of intact forest and a further 23 100 hectares of heavily logged forest. Using the excellent detailed rainforest vegetation maps of rainforest scientists Webb and Tracey, we estimate that in northern Queensland there are 165 000 hectares of their types 8 (Simple Notophyll Vine Forest) and 9 (Simple Notophyll Vine-fern Forest).

In North Queensland from Mt Finnegan to Ravenshoe this type of rainforest occurs on the poorer yellow earth soils derived from schists and granites at elevations of 400 to 1000 metres. Amongst the canopy trees are three species of *Ceratopetalum*, the most common being blood-in-the-bark (*Ceratopetalum succirubrum*). Commonly overtopping the main canopy are scattered trees of black kauri pine (*Agathis microstachya*).

In central coastal Queensland on Kroombit Tops, south-west of Gladstone, along the creeks there is a warm temperate rainforest characterised by coachwood (*Ceratopetalum apetalum*) and callicoma (*Callicoma serratifolia*) on soils derived from rhyolite and trachyte.

Moving southwards, suitable cool moist conditions are not encountered again until along the New South Wales border, at Daves Creek and Lightning Falls in Lamington National Park. Here, on the poorer soils derived from rhyolite lavas of the ancient Mt Warning volcano, are more forests dominated by coachwood. This rainforest type occurs again on the remnant southern flanks on the Nightcap Range and on the equivalent rocks of the central volcanic core itself midway up Mt Warning. To the west along the McPherson Range, where influenced by the slightly better soils from the Mt Barney series of rhyolite lavas, the major tree is no longer coachwood but is the crabapple (*Schizomeria ovata*) as on Levers Plateau, Mount Glennie and the southern slopes of Mt Lindesay. This close relationship between crabapple and coachwood and the parent rock is beautifully illustrated on the granites south-east of Tenterfield, where warm temperate rainforest dominated by coachwood is found on the poorer soils derived from adamellite, whilst crabapple is on the slightly richer soils from the adamellite porphyrite.

Further south, on the same adamellite soils, is the Willowie Scrub of Washpool National Park, consisting of 3000 hectares of pristine coachwood forest — the largest intact area of coachwood rainforest in Australia. Significant areas, much of which have been logged, occur in Cangai State Forest, on Mt Hyland, the eastern Dorrigo, Styx River State Forest, Carrai Plateau and the headwaters of

Tree fern grove in a warm temperate forest at Barrington Tops.

the Hastings River west of Port Macquarie. The parent rocks are either metamorphics or granites. In the Dorrigo area, as in North Queensland, there are often native pines such as hoop pine (*Araucaria cunninghamii*) overtopping the main canopy.

At Barrington Tops the coachwood suballiance is confined to poorer sandstone areas such as Chichester State Forest, whilst the somewhat more fertile mudstones with basaltic enrichment from above support crabapple, sassafras (*Doryphora sassafras*), corkwood (*Caldcluvia paniculosa*) and prickly ash (*Orites excelsa*).

South of the Hunter River the warm temperate rainforest dominated by coachwood occurs on the moister southern sides of the higher mountains as on Mt Monundilla and Mt Coricudgy or deep in the slot canyons on sandstone and shale. The exposed sandstone plateau with its frequent fires effectively restricts the rainforest to these refuges. In the Blue Mountains it occurs in the gully heads of the gorges with a moist south to east aspect, such as beneath Horseshoe Falls at Govett's Leap and at Wentworth Falls. It also occupies a similar niche along the Illawarra escarpment, often on the shales beneath the sandstone. South from the Hunter River to its southern limit at Currowan Creek near Batemans Bay, crabapple, corkwood and prickly ash are replaced as the major subsidiary canopy trees by sassafras and particularly lilly pilly (*Acmena smithii*).

From Batemans Bay to East Gippsland, Victoria, lilly pilly is the major suballiance below 500 metres altitude, where it is restricted to narrow sheltered creek banks that are protected from all but the worst bushfires. Typical examples are in Dampier State Forest, Wadbilliga National Park and at Nadgee near the Victorian border. At higher altitudes and on better soils it forms a mixed canopy with pinkwood (*Eucryphia moorei*), whilst on drier sites and poorer soils it is associated with grey myrtle (*Backhousia myrtifolia*). On the better volcanic soils such as the basalt on the Liverpool Range, the latite at Minnamurra Falls and the monzonite at Mt Dromedary, there is an intergrading of subtropical–warm temperate rainforests characterised by lilly pilly, giant stinging tree (*Dendrocnide excelsa*) and figs (*Ficus rubiginosa* and *F. obliqua*).

Above altitudes of 700–1000 metres on the central and north coasts of New South Wales, coachwood cannot withstand the exposure and is replaced by sassafras. On basaltic soils as at Mt Spirabo near Tenterfield and Mt Coriaday in the Hunter Valley, it is associated with brown possumwood (*Quintinia sieberi*) or, on less fertile soils, with crabapple as at Gibraltar Range.

Whereas there are warm temperate–subtropical rainforest intergrades south of the Hunter River involving lilly pilly, there are equi-

Fruiting bodies of rainbow fungus (*Trametes versicolor*).

Coachwood trunks and tree fern fronds.

valent intergrades of coachwood north of the Hunter Valley with either booyongs (*Argyrodendron actinophyllum* and A. *trifoliolatum*) at altitudes below 650 metres or with yellow carabeen (*Sloanea woollsii*) at higher altitudes. Typical examples are Hogans Scrub near Tumbulgum and Washpool National Park respectively. In addition, coachwood south of the Hunter River can intergrade with such subtropical rainforest elements as tamarind (*Diploglottis cunninghamii*) and red cedar (*Toona australis*) as at Wheeny Creek in Wollemi National Park and Walker's Garden, Royal National Park. In all these sites the intergrade has been possible because of the enriched soil, thereby allowing some subtropical rainforest species to occur.

STRUCTURE

In contrast to the tropical and subtropical rainforests, the canopy is generally of even height and commonly up to 30 metres above ground. Because the leaves are mainly simple and rather small and the trees are closely spaced, the individual crowns appear uniform and densely packed in contrast to the turbulent surface of the subtropical and tropical rainforests. However, it is not uncommon to find scattered much-taller trees in some areas, which may be merely remnants of an older open forest such as eucalypts or brush box (*Lophostemon confertus*); or may be a true component of the ongoing rainforest such as brush box once again and various conifers of the family Araucariaceae such as hoop pine in the Dorrigo district of New South Wales, kauri pines in North Queensland, and klinki pine (*Araucaria hunsteinii*) in New Guinea.

Warm temperate rainforest is generally not as tall as subtropical rainforest, and it possesses only two tree layers. The number of species in the upper layer or canopy may be only up to fifteen but is sometimes as low as three.

The trunks usually do not reach the huge proportions of those in the subtropical rainforest, nor do they exhibit pronounced buttressing. Yellow carabeen (*Sloanea woollsii*) is a notable exception. There is usually a preponderance of trees with smooth grey barks such as coachwood, callicoma and prickly ash, often spattered with colourful lichen patches – rather than the cloak of climbers and large bracket epiphytes so typical of subtropical and tropical rainforests. There are, however, some rough-barked trees such as hoop and kauri pines, brush box, crabapple, sassafras and lilly pilly.

The canopy leaves are smaller than in the subtropical rainforest, commonly between 7.5 and 12.5 centimetres long, but becoming even smaller with increasing altitude where sassafras predominates. They are mostly toothed and simple rather than compound.

The fronds of a cabbage tree palm (*Livistona australis*).

158

A mosaic of cloud mist and warm temperate rainforest canopy.

Birthplace of fresh and crystal clear nutritious waters.

Brush turkey (*Alectura lathami*) roost at night in the safety of the subcanopy.

A male brush turkey uses displays to induce a female to lay her eggs in his nest mound.

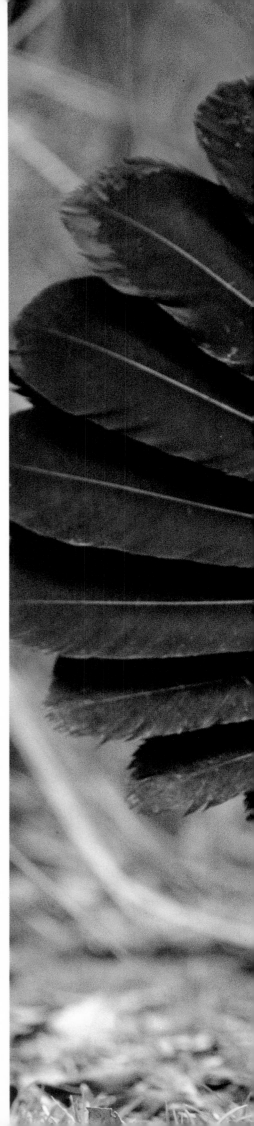

A brush turkey, its plumage fluffed up after heavy rain, feeds upon fruits and animals on the forest floor.

The thick woody vines or ropes of the subtropical rainforest are less obvious; but there are many more slender and wiry vines present, including the lawyer canes (*Calamus* spp.).

Large epiphytes, because of the preponderance of smooth-barked trees, are found mainly up in the crowns rather than further down on the trunks as in the tropical and subtropical rainforests. There are also fewer species present.

Tall palms may be common in gully situations, and smaller palm species such as midginbil (*Linospadix* spp.) are well represented in the understorey of forests from northern New South Wales to North Queensland. In addition to tree ferns there is a good ground cover of smaller ferns.

At higher elevations with increasing rainfall, the forest type is temperate rainforest, in which the canopy is even more simple and the trunks are often obscured by the dense growth of mosses, ferns and lichens.

FLORA

Woody vines seek purchase among lichen-clad creek-edge boulders at Mt Dromedary.

Floristically the warm temperate rainforest is less diverse than subtropical and tropical rainforests, but it contains many primitive and restricted families and genera, thereby indicating its great antiquity. The principal families are Cunoniaceae, Escalloniaceae, Proteaceae, Lauraceae, Myrtaceae and Atherospermataceae, which are also well represented in the cool moist rainforests of New Zealand, New Caledonia and South America (all sections of the old Gondwanaland supercontinent). Genera common to Australia and South America include *Orites*, *Lomatia* and *Aristotelia*, whilst closely related genera are found to *Oreocallis*, *Tasmannia* and *Pseudoweinmannia*. There are links with New Zealand through *Agathis*, *Caldcluvia*, *Quintinia* and *Beilschmiedia*; and with New Caledonia via *Vesselowskya*, *Quintinia*, *Agathis*, *Corokia* and *Uromyrtus*.

Along the Australian east coast there are three high mountain areas close to the sea and hence receiving very high rainfall: in the south is the Dorrigo Plateau, rising to 1563 metres at Point Lookout; near the Queensland border is Mt Warning, now 1157 metres high but originally twice that height according to Dr P. Solomon; and in North Queensland are Mts Bellenden Ker and Bartle Frere, reaching 1600 metres. During periods of great climatic change such as arid or hot cycles, these three mountain areas acted as fortresses for the embattled rainforests, which would have been eliminated elsewhere.

The native honeysuckle (*Triunia youngiana*) is found today only at these three areas; and there are many examples where the major tree species common to both the Dorrigo and Mt Warning areas

Cabbage tree palms and tree ferns at Barrington Tops.

Colourful new leaf growth of Macleay laurel (*Anopteris macleayana*) breaks the monotony of greenness.

have a closely related species in North Queensland. For example, coachwood is replaced by blood-in-the-bark, tree waratah (*Oreocallis pinnata*) by pink silky oak (*Oreocallis wickhamii*), sassafras by northern sassafras (*Doryphora aromatica*), and crabapple by another crabapple (*Schizomeria whitei*). Several species are common to both areas such as brush box, lilly pilly, prickly ash and bolwarra (*Eupomatia laurina*). Within New South Wales there are species confined to the Dorrigo and Mt Warning refuges such as tree waratah, southern quassia (*Quassia* sp. aff. *bidwillii*) and Dorrigo plum (*Endiandra introrsa*). It is of interest that although there is no obvious visible difference between the Dorrigo plum at Dorrigo and the plum growing on the Nightcap Range section of Mt Warning, recent chemical analysis carried out on the leaves has shown considerable differences, presumably as a result of the long period of isolation.

There are many primitive genera in the family Proteaceae in northern Queensland such as *Placospermum* and *Sphalmium*, which indicate either that this is their birthplace or that they have died out elsewhere and have been able to find refuge only there. Dr Christophel recently found a fossilised flower spike and associated leaves at Anglesea in southern Victoria which are closely related to *Musgravea* and *Austromuellera*, now only known from the warm temperate rainforests in North Queensland. This suggests that some of these ancient Proteaceae genera may have extended at least as far as southern Victoria 50 million years ago. Drs Johnson and Briggs had earlier regarded *Musgravea* and *Austromuellera* as being the ancestral stock of the banksias, now so widespread throughout Australia; and the restriction of these ancestral genera to a small wet cool mountain area in North Queensland was puzzling. Further evidence of this early widespread distribution of warm temperate rainforest in southern Australia is the finding of a fossil fruit near Adelaide, also about 50 million years old, which is remarkably similar to that of present-day coachwood.

FAUNA

Considering the remarkable diversity and antiquity of the flora of the warm temperate rainforest of Australia, particularly in the major refugia such as the high mountains of north-east Queensland and the Mt Warning system to the south, it is not surprising that the fauna is of special interest.

Mammals of the Atherton uplands and Thornton Peak subregions have been discussed in Chapter 2. Many species are either unique to this area or are extremely isolated — the nearest populations being hundreds or even thousands of kilometres to the south — such

Cascading waters in Dorrigo National Park.

The epiphytic crow's nest ferns (*Asplenium australasicum*) grow on boulders as well as on trees.

The flood waters of torrential rains accumulate tree logs in a rocky creek bed.

Rainbow fungi, seen here in fruit, digest fallen dead wood.

Light cloud mist silhouettes warm temperate forest.

Common ringtail possum (*Pseudocheirus peregrinus pulcher*).

The mountain brushtail possum (*Trichosaurus caninus*).

as the brown antechinus, spotted-tailed quoll and white-footed dunnart. Whereas these three species are not restricted to rainforests, they probably use them as refuges in unfavourable times such as during bushfires or longer climatic changes. Similarly the pademelons, parma wallaby (*Macropus parma*) and potoroo (*Potorous tridactylus*) inhabit the rainforest margin, often feeding in the adjoining open forest but sheltering in the rainforest.

The other faunal group that has been well studied in the rainforest is the birds. Because of their great mobility, they range freely through subtropical, warm temperate and cool temperate rainforests as well as into the adjoining wet sclerophyll or open forest according to the availability of food. For this reason the fruit-eating pigeons are more commonly found in the subtropical and tropical rainforests where a higher percentage of plant species have juicy edible fruits. Such distinctive birds as the superb lyrebird, scrub turkey, green catbird and satin bowerbird (which were described in the previous chapter on subtropical rainforests) are equally common in the warm temperate rainforest of New South Wales.

The small shy but very noisy rufous scrub-bird inhabits dense thickets in the cool mountain forests from the Barrington Tops to the Queensland border. Although it is most frequently heard in the cool and warm temperate rainforests, it does dwell in the subtropical rainforest and even the wet sclerophyll forest if the undergrowth is sufficiently dense. Because of its habitat it tends to hop rather than fly and is rarely seen on the wing. This reduced mobility has given rise to two populations with different calls, one on the McPherson and Gibraltar Ranges and the other to the south in the Dorrigo, Hastings and Barrington areas. These populations are correlated with a major floristic barrier caused by the dry open forests of the Mann and Nymboida valleys.

The reptiles and amphibians of the warm temperate rainforest are less well known. There is a decrease in the number of species with increasing altitude and latitude. Species living in the subtropical rainforest, such as the southern angle-headed dragon and the pouched frog, are found also in the warm temperate rainforest; but whereas the southern angle-headed dragon is more common in the subtropical rainforest because of its generic links with south-east Asia, the pouched frog prefers the mossy floor of the cool temperate rainforest at high altitudes. This frog, with the interesting brood pouches of the male, is the only species in its genus. It has been recorded from only three areas, namely the Mt Warning system, Washpool and Dorrigo. These three sites would once have been on the north–south corridor of cool temperate rainforest; and whereas

Bangalow palm frond (*foreground*) and cabbage tree palm (*background*).

Rain sparkles on leaf and vine cane surfaces.

the two end localities still consist of this rainforest type, that at Washpool is now *warm* temperate rainforest.

Other faunal groups are poorly known. A faunal survey in 1975–6 of east coast rainforests by the Australian Museum revealed that more than 60 per cent of the species of spiders collected were unnamed, as were 57 per cent of the molluscs. Hence it is impossible to assess their true scientific importance at this stage. For example, the large snail, *Hedleyella falconeri*, with a shell up to 8 centimetres in diameter, which is confined to the subtropical and warm temperate rainforests of southern Queensland and northern New South Wales, is amongst the largest land snails in the world. The other members of this family occur in Madagascar, Sri Lanka and Chile (which were all segments of the ancient Gondwanaland supercontinent). Thoughts of distant days are of no concern to the noisy pitta as it pounds the large shell against its special anvil stone to expose the succulent feast within.

HISTORY OF HUMAN USE

There is little recorded use by the Aborigines of warm temperate rainforest, possibly because its cool damp conditions were rather uncomfortable and most of its major plant species did not produce edible fruits or seeds. Game was not plentiful. However, the rainforest margin was more productive, yielding pademelon wallabies, goannas, carpet snakes, possums, fruits such as lilly pilly and wild ginger (*Alpinea caerulea*), and tubers such as yam (*Dioscorea transversa*) and orange vine (*Eustrephus latifolius*).

After the arrival of the British, logging and clearing of rainforest for farming was concentrated firstly upon the rich alluvial lowland flats of the larger rivers, where timber such as red cedar could be rafted to the waiting sailing vessels. The fertile basaltic plateaux were next in line: Atherton, the Big Scrub, Dorrigo and Comboyne. All these areas carried tropical and subtropical rainforest. As the availability of this land became exhausted, attention was focused on the adjoining warm temperate rainforest and eucalypt forests on the poorer soils derived from metamorphic rocks.

In North Queensland, land was first offered for sale at Kuranda and Julatten in 1885, and the railway to link these areas with Cairns was built in 1891. A total of 9550 hectares was sold, of which 1400 hectares had been cleared by 1925. However, the dream of a thriving dairying community turned sour as it was later realised that this magnificent rainforest was growing on a poor yellow clay; and it relied for its nutrients upon a rapid cycle of litter decay and mineral uptake by the surface roots. When the forest was cleared, the nut-

Bracket fungi attack a dead tree stump supporting a bird's nest fern (*Asplenium nidus*) above.

1 The reproductive spores of this fungus are held in the blackish slime.

2 This shell-shaped fungus is a particularly common wood-digesting species.

3 A star fungus about to open up.

4 A gilled fungus fruits from the trunk of a dead tree.

5 The young fruiting body of a rainbow fungus.

Decomposing leaves provide nutrition for countless
aquatic debris-feeding invertebrate animals.

Falls with *Sticherus* fan ferns (*at bottom left*).

rients were quickly leached out of the soil by the torrential rains, and the pastures began to fail. Today much of this land, having been abandoned, is returning once again to forest aided by an umbrella of wattles. The local economy has switched from milking cows to tourism.

The eastern Dorrigo has a similar history. To the north of the fertile basaltic plateau there were extensive tracts of warm temperate rainforest consisting of coachwood and towering hoop pine, interspersed with magnificent eucalypt forest. Prospective farmers were impressed by the fine forest growth and the high rainfall, but they overlooked the poor soil. The rainforest was easier to clear than the eucalypt forest, being softer, and the stumps soon rotted out. Hence in 1909 a Lands Department subdivision offered 142 farms each of 60–130 hectares. In a brochure entitled *The Guide to the Dorrigo Shire* in 1917 it was enthusiastically stated that: 'there are large tracts of country here where thousands of industrious dairy farmers could be placed on small areas which would amply maintain them . . . It is unquestionably due to the fact that Dorrigo is one of the finest watered areas in Australia, if not in the world, that dairying on the plateau is such a phenomenal success.'

'Diggers' returned from the Great War were settled on the land under soldier–settler schemes, only to slide into bankruptcy. In 1926 Lane-Poole assessed the situation thus: 'As settlement scheme it is almost a complete failure, there being only 135 left out of the 160 who took up blocks, and these are not making a living out of the production of the soil, but by labouring in timber and other industries of the locality . . . Not more than 8 of the settlers are using the land for dairying or farming.'

The current situation is that dairying has ceased, many abandoned farms are slowly regenerating with various colonising species such as tick bush (*Helichrysum diosmifolium*), wattles, and callicoma, and the remainder are commonly beef-cattle 'hobby farms'.

The major areas of warm temperate rainforest in New South Wales are the Nightcap Range, Forestland–Washpool–Cangai, Mt Hyland–eastern Dorrigo, Carrai and upper Hastings, all of which have been heavily logged in part for their valuable coachwood timber. Up until World War Two, only the very best trees were taken, and hence the disturbance in the forest was not very great. However, during the war there was a great demand for this timber for rifles and as plywood for the bodies of Mosquito bombers. This resulted in heavy logging and disturbance, which even increased after the war during the building boom. The use of tractors and heavy trucks enabled previously inaccessible areas to be logged. The Forestry

The diamond python (*Morelia spilotes*).

The roots of a tree can literally tear rocks apart.

The fruits and fronds of the walking-stick palm (*Linospadix monostachyus*).

Commission found that the remaining coachwood trees after logging showed extensive dieback and even death. There was therefore no advantage in leaving them; and so it was decided in the Wauchope area to fell all usable trees and to replant with coachwood seedlings. Unfortunately this species requires the protection of other trees and shrubs for its early growth, and the plantings were largely unsuccessful. Eucalypts were therefore planted instead. This is why nearly 50 per cent of the remaining warm temperate rainforest in New South Wales has been considerably disturbed. In most areas, coachwood will eventually form a forest once more after going through the laborious appropriate stages of succession, but it has been calculated that it may take 200 years to grow a tree to a size suitable for logging and it would be many centuries more before it reaches the end of its lifespan.

South of the Hunter River there are not substantial tracts of warm temperate rainforest except on Mt Coricudgy which has been very heavily logged and burnt. There are many patches of rainforest in narrow gullies, but these are being gradually destroyed because of their use as firebreaks. Whereas north of the Hunter River the weather pattern shows maximum rainfall in summer, further south there tend to be longer hot dry periods at that time resulting in more intense wildfires. Although the rainforest is sensitive to fire, it is often deliberately used as a firebreak with predictable results. Many of the South Coast rainforest remnants have been repeatedly burnt, reducing the trees to mere props for tangles of vines.

Conservation Status

In terms of total area conserved today, the warm temperate rainforest has fared better than subtropical and tropical rainforests in regions of potentially prime agricultural land. Despite this, logging continues unabated in northern Queensland which, although not destroying the rainforest, does alter its structure for an indeterminate period depending upon the criteria considered important.

In New South Wales where the bulk of this rainforest occurs, 87.2 per cent of the intact rainforest is now in reserves, of which 80 per cent is under the control of the National Parks and Wildlife Service. As recently as October 1982 when the government made its decision on rainforest logging, only 42.1 per cent of all intact warm temperate rainforest was in reserves. Considerable progress has therefore been made; but of the 17 suballiances of plants recognised by the author in 1984, eight were considered to be inadequately reserved over their full geographic range. Since then, action has been taken on three of these deficiencies, whilst the remainder are in state forests in dis-

Palms, ferns and lianes.

tricts where there is no rainforest logging permitted. Given a continuance of the present government rainforest policy, the conservation of the warm temperate rainforest in New South Wales north of Sydney could be regarded as satisfactory.

However, the fragmented creek-side remnants on the South Coast are being steadily eroded by wildfires, probably aggravated by the high fuel levels resulting from logging in the sclerophyll forests. A survey of these areas was undertaken in 1982, using aerial photographs taken just before the disastrous 1980 fires. In many cases, the rainforest has completely disappeared. So the practice of regarding these rainforest strips as 'green firebreaks' is becoming less effective and must be replaced by a deliberate effort to protect the rainforest from these fires by strip burning.

Red-eyed tree frog (Litoria chloris)

6
COOL TEMPERATE RAINFORESTS: NEW SOUTH WALES

KEVIN MILLS

COOL TEMPERATE rainforests are characterised by an abundance of ferns and mosses and lack many typical rainforest features that commonly come to mind such as vines, epiphytes and palms. Leaf sizes of shrubs and trees are small, and species diversity is generally low. Structurally, these forests are termed microphyll moss or fern forests. In contrast to subtropical and warm temperate rainforests which can also be found over parts of the same geographical range, cool temperate rainforests have only a few tree species and the structural complexity of the forest is far less diverse.

The atmosphere of cool temperate rainforests is one of solemnness and is often referred to as being 'cathedral-like'. It has a mysteriously impressive character and quietness. The flash of colourful birds and butterflies and the impression of the vibrant life of the more tropical rainforests are largely absent.

The cool temperate rainforests in New South Wales are dominated by either of two tree species, both virtually restricted to the state, but with close relatives in other parts of Australia and elsewhere. In southern New South Wales, plumwood or pinkwood (*Eucryphia moorei*) dominates the cool temperate forests; in the north, negrohead beech (*Nothofagus moorei*) is the dominant tree.

Eucryphia is a genus of seven species, found in Chile and Australia. The four Australian species are found in Tasmania (two species), Queensland and New South Wales. Plumwood is distri-

WASHPOOL

DORRIGO PLATEAU • COFFS HARBOUR

NEW SOUTH WALES

BANDA-BANDA
BARRINGTON TOPS • PORT MACQUARIE
NAT. PK.

WOLLONGONG

COOL TEMPERATE RAINFORESTS
OF NEW SOUTH WALES

MT. DROMEDARY
• NAROOMA

buted along the coastal ranges of southern New South Wales from the Howe Range on the Victorian border in the south to the gullies of the Woronora Plateau, west of Wollongong, in the north. This species thus has a latitudinal range from about 34°30′ to 37°30′ S.

Nothofagus, like *Eucryphia*, is a southern hemisphere genus, consisting of some 35 species found mainly in Australia, New Zealand and South America. The New South Wales species, N. *moorei*, is found from the Barrington Tops at its southern limit of distribution to just over the Queensland border, a latitudinal range from 28° to 32° S.

In the Blue Mountains west of Sydney, neither plumwood (which has its distribution to the south) nor negrohead beech (which extends to the north) is present, even though there are potentially suitable sites at altitudes over 1000 metres. Their absence from this area of potential overlap has likely occurred because of the long existence of very dry corridors to the north (the Hunter Valley) and the south (the Wollondilly River valley). On high-altitude basalt soils in the Blue Mountains area, such as at Mt Wilson, the rainforest is of a cool–warm temperate character. The species common here are coachwood (*Ceratopetalum apetalum*), sassafras (*Doryphora sassafras*), and cool temperate species such as southern sassafras (*Atherosperma moschatum*) and possumwood (*Quintinia sieberi*). The only Australian region where species of *Eucryphia* and *Nothofagus* co-exist is in Tasmania — where they are the dominant trees of the cool temperate rainforests.

THE EUCRYPHIA RAINFORESTS

Unlike other rainforest types such as the subtropical forests, *Eucryphia* cool temperate rainforest does not cover extensive areas of country. Like most of the rainforest in southern New South Wales, this type has generally developed as small patches in well-protected locations away from wildfire and drier aspects. As the term 'cool temperate' suggests, plumwood forest reaches its best development at high altitudes where temperatures are low. Here, also, moisture loss is limited and rainfall high. In addition these areas are commonly subjected to fogs which add to the available moisture and reduce evaporation rates.

At their highest altitudinal occurrences, stands of plumwood occur in more exposed locations. But at lower altitudes and at lower extremes of rainfall, they occur only in deep gullies; here the trees may grow in a narrow band along a stream. In the Illawarra district at its northern limit of distribution, plumwood is generally found only above 500 metres elevation, although it can be found to lower altitudes in deeply incised gorges. Temperatures in such gorges are often low because of cold air drainage from adjacent high ground.

The trunks of these pinkwood (*Eucryphia moorei*) are particularly rich in epiphytic mosses and lichens.

Further south the species tends to occur at lower altitudes. For example, at Nadgee Nature Reserve on the New South Wales–Victorian border it occurs in gullies at just over 100 metres.

A number of plant communities associated with *Eucryphia* can be recognised over its range. On the Woronora Plateau plumwood is associated with coachwood, with sassafras and featherwood (*Polyosma cunninghamii*) as secondary tree species. Ferns and mosses are also common.

Plumwood is frequently associated with sassafras at lower altitudes or forms nearly pure stands at the highest altitudes. In the south, lilly pilly (*Acmena smithii*) is a common associate. Other species with which it is associated are mountain blueberry (*Elaeocarpus holopetalus*), southern sassafras and possumwood. Possumwood has the unusual habit of germinating epiphytically on the trunk of a tree fern. The seedling is not parasitic but uses the root mass of the tree fern as a convenient germination site from where it grows to the ground and eventually develops as a normal tree. The tree fern, which may fall under the weight, usually survives and regrows, often at an irregular angle. Occasionally other trees such as plumwood also germinate on tree ferns in this fashion.

In the wetter areas, soft green carpets of filmy ferns (*Hymenophyllum* spp.) cover rocks, tree ferns and tree trunks. Mosses are ubiquitous, delicate green fronds clothing damp rocks, or long tangled masses festooning tree branches.

Eucryphia forests usually occur as a mosaic of small patches amongst tall eucalypt forest (wet sclerophyll forest), although other rainforest communities are sometimes found adjacent. For example, in the Barren Grounds area near its northern limit, plumwood forest is found as a narrow band on the upper slopes of the Illawarra escarpment. At medium altitudes below this, warm temperate rainforest is found; and at lower altitudes still, mainly on volcanic soil, subtropical rainforest occurs.

An interesting gradation in rainforest types can also be seen at Mt Dromedary Flora Reserve, south of Narooma on the South Coast. Here the volcanic monzonite soil supports a diverse subtropical rainforest in the gullies at lower altitudes, and on the slopes of the summit, at 700 metres elevation, there are stands of plumwood cool temperate rainforest. The diversity of the lower rainforest community with its vines, epiphytes, palms, trees such as figs (*Ficus* spp.) and stinging tree (*Dendrocnide excelsa*) and dense ground cover of small shrubs and ferns, contrasts sharply with the simpler high-altitude stands. Tree ferns are common only at the higher elevations on the mountain; the species found are the prickly tree fern (*Cyathea leich-*

A crimson rosella tail-feather joins other leaf-litter debris.

hardtiana) and the soft tree fern (*Dicksonia antarctica*). Two notable plants which occur here are the blanket bush (*Bedfordia arborescens*), with its large soft leaves, and the showy musk daisy bush (*Olearia argophylla*) which produces masses of small white daisy flowers. These species occur in the cooler mountain forests in the south of the state, including the edges of rainforest.

The brown pigeon (*Macropygia amboinensis*)

THE NOTHOFAGUS RAINFORESTS

Nothofagus moorei cool temperate rainforests have a discontinuous distribution over their range, generally occurring over about 800 metres altitude, but in a few places as low as 500 metres. Beech is commonly associated with coachwood, except at the highest altitudes where it forms fairly pure stands – for example, at Barrington Tops in central New South Wales. Sassafras is also a common associate species, along with prickly ash (*Orites excelsa*) and small-leaved laurel (*Cryptocarya foveolata*). Tree ferns are also common, particularly the soft tree fern which is distributed throughout the cooler rainforest types including those in Tasmania. One plant of interest is the beech orchid (*Dendrobium falcorostrum*) which grows as an epiphyte on negrohead beech trees. The flowers of this orchid, which can number up to 20 on a single raceme, are white with purple markings and are highly fragrant.

At its best development, beech forest is dominated by huge gnarled moss-covered trunks usually with multiple stems consisting of suckers of various ages. (This habit of multiple-stemmed trees, together with a lack of seedlings on the forest floor, is also shared with plumwood.) The uncluttered floor of a beech forest is carpeted in a thick layer of the fallen golden and rust leaves. Sunrays piercing the canopy and illuminating the massive old trunks justify the frequent use of the cathedral analogy.

At Barrington Tops *Nothofagus*-dominated rainforest merges with cool subtropical rainforest at about 900 metres. Here many other species are found joining the community, including prickly ash, crab apple (*Schizomeria ovata*) and rosewood (*Dysoxylum fraserianum*). One species that catches the eye is a restricted shrub, the broad-leaved pepperbush (*Tasmannia purpurescens*), which is only found in the Barrington Tops area. (This species is usually found on the edge of the rainforest communities or within eucalpyt forest at higher altitudes.) The plants stand out against a green backdrop, with their clusters of purple berries and red and green leaves.

Coachwood becomes a common associate of beech in areas to the north, such as in the upper Forbes River valley and the Mt Banda Banda area west of Port Macquarie, along the New England escarp-

Tree ferns flourish on the lighter forest floor of cool temperate rainforests.

Cooler damp rainforests are particularly suitable for lush moss growth.

Dawsonia moss occurs in the cooler rainforest areas of south-eastern Australia.

ment, and in the gullies of the Dorrigo Plateau west of Coffs Harbour. In all areas, only at the very highest altitudes are there pure stands of *Nothofagus*.

A seemingly anomalous situation occurs, for example, at Barrington Tops and on the Dorrigo Plateau where adjacent to beech forest can be found areas of subalpine woodland. In these areas, which contribute significantly to the contrasting scenery of the Barrington Tops National Park, can be found snow grass (*Poa.* sp.) and the snow gum (*Eucalyptus pauciflora*).

WILDLIFE

Unlike many other rainforest communities, the animal fauna of the cool temperate rainforests is low in diversity. Furthermore, there are very few animal species that are totally restricted to cool temperate rainforest in New South Wales. 'Typical' rainforest bird species such as the fruit pigeons are absent from these cooler forests. This is not surprising, for there are very few trees producing the fleshy fruits required by these birds.

The best place to look for birds and other wildlife is often the edges of the rainforest, where light penetrates and therefore denser, more diverse plant communities are found, offering the food and shelter required. Here we shall consider only a few of the more interesting and/or typical animals.

The rufous scrub-bird (*Atrichornis rufescens*) is a threatened species which was once more widespread in north-eastern New South Wales. It is a secretive bird of the undergrowth and is found only in isolated populations at higher altitudes between Barrington Tops and just over the Queensland border to Mt Mistake. Sightings have been recorded in shrubby edges of cool temperate rainforest. It has been suggested that the species may be extinct below 400 metres altitude.

A widespread species in the wet forests of south-eastern Australia is White's thrush (*Zoothera dauma*). This ground-dwelling bird can be found throughout the range of cool temperate rainforest, including Tasmania. Its dappled brown plumage provides a perfect camouflage amongst the forest floor litter of leaves and logs, where it seeks insects and worms.

Two of the 'red' robins can be found in the cool temperate rainforests: the rose robin (*Petroica rosea*) and the pink robin (*P. rodinogaster*). The former is found throughout the range of mainland cool temperate rainforest, whereas the latter is restricted to southern New South Wales, Victoria and Tasmania. Both are found in the wetter forests over their ranges, including the cool temperate rainforest.

The olive whistler (*Pachycephala olivacea*) is of interest not only for

View of rain-laden sky at sunset from Mt Dromedary.

Bracken ferns dominate the undergrowth of this cool temperate rainforest.

The canopy of cool temperate rainforests is very much sparser than tropical rainforest.

its reputation as a songster but also because it has different habitat preferences over its range in south-eastern Australia. In the north the birds inhabit the high-altitude rainforests north of Barrington Tops to the Queensland border, while in the south it can be found in open woodlands such as those in Kosciusko National Park.

The reptile and amphibian fauna of the cool temperate rainforests is quite limited in comparison with other habitats. Of interest are three species of frogs, noted by scientists Barker and Grigg, which are confined to the cool mountainous rainforests of the McPherson Range and nearby areas. The first, Loveridge's frog (*Kyarranus loveridgei*), is a small frog 25mm long, found in the litter of the forest floor. A related species, K. *kundagungan*, is found in similar habitat just over the Queensland border and was discovered only in 1975. The third species is the quaintly named hip pocket frog (*Assa darlingtoni*) This tiny (20 mm) frog is unique in that the male cares for its eggs and larvae by carrying them in 'pouches' located on either side of its flanks. This phenomenon is unique amongst Australian frogs.

CONSERVATION STATUS

Of the many rainforest types found in New South Wales, the cool temperate types are the least disturbed by human agencies and are now the most adequately conserved in appropriate reserves. In general the location of these rainforests — that is, fragmented and at high altitude, inaccessible and on steeply sloping ground — in addition to their lack of significant timber species, has meant that compared with other rainforest types little has been destroyed.

Some areas have been affected by logging, often of adjacent forests rather than the rainforest itself, and to a lesser extent through clearing. For example, minor clearing of *Eucryphia* forest occurred on the Robertson Plateau to the south-west of Wollongong (most of this rainforest was warm temperate/subtropical in character): and gold mining in the 1850s affected the stands on the summit of Mt Dromedary. *Nothofagus* rainforest has generally escaped large-scale disturbance but has been affected to some extent by logging, clearing and fire. Where coachwood and beech grow together, coachwood logging has resulted in wind and light penetration which has in turn caused dieback in the beech crowns.

The area of *intact* New South Wales cool temperate rainforest has been estimated at some 18 000 hectares. Thus cool temperate rainforest types account for some 9.3 per cent of the estimated 193 000 hectares of intact rainforest remaining in the state. Three-quarters of this area is associated with *Nothofagus* rainforest types in the north

Ancient tree ferns witness the slow breakdown of a fallen forest giant.

A tree fern grove flourishes on particularly good litter.

A moss fruit capsule.

of the state, although because of the fragmented locations of *Eucryphia*-dominated forests their estimated area is probably an underestimate of the actual area.

Almost all of the cool temperate rainforest identified by the Forestry Commission is on land controlled by the Crown, the major authorities being the Forestry Commission and the National Parks and Wildlife Service. Some 45 per cent of this rainforest type, since the recent transfers of areas to the Service, is within conservation reserves, including Flora Reserves controlled by the Forestry Commission.

Other authorities control smaller but nonetheless significant areas of forest. For example, at the northern limit of *Eucryphia* rainforest most stands are within the water catchment area of the Metropolitan Water Sewerage and Drainage Board (Sydney). Similarly at the southern limit of the distribution of *Nothofagus moorei* important stands occur within the Chichester Catchment under the control of the Hunter District Water Board. Sympathetic management practices need to be formulated to protect these rainforest stands and the other natural values in these areas.

Except for the need for preservation in suitable reserves of a number of the more restricted associations (for example, the *Eucryphia moorei–Acmena smithii* association at the southern limit of *E. moorei*) the future of the cool temperate rainforests in New South Wales looks comparatively secure.

Threats do arise from wildfire, as most of this rainforest type occurs in patches over its range, usually associated with the more fire-prone eucalypt forests. Threats to these forests may in future come from the increased visitor pressures, including increased risk of fire, brought about by the heightening of interest by the public in visiting and recreating in these rainforests.

Cool temperate rainforests are generally well preserved in the national parks system in New South Wales and are accessible to the general public throughout their range. *Eucryphia* rainforest can be seen at Mt Dromedary Flora Reserve, Clyde Mountain, Budawang National Park and Barren Grounds Nature Reserve, all in southern New South Wales. *Nothofagus* rainforest can be seen at Barrington Tops National Park, New England National Park, Dorrigo National Park and Lamington National Park (Queensland).

A very old stand of pinkwood in Monga State Forest, southern New South Wales.

7

COOL TEMPERATE RAINFORESTS:

TASMANIA AND VICTORIA

TIM O'LOUGHLIN AND ROBERT BLAKERS

COOL TEMPERATURE rainforest seems to be forgotten when we think of Australia's rainforests, yet in area it constitutes a quarter of all rainforests remaining in Australia today.

The essence of cool temperate rainforest lies in its cool moistness; the riot of colour and species diversity found in tropical rainforest is replaced with balanced simplicity. This, the most southerly of all rainforests, has a 'Tolkien-like' atmosphere, where the trunks of the myrtle are soft and moss covered, the sassafras is tall and graceful with long upright branches and smooth mottled bark. The forest floor is thick brown peat and gives softly to the tread. Delicate ferns and intricate lichens grow vigorously from every surface. The scents are crisp and earthy. Except for the vivid brightness of fungi or the rare flower, or the brown of the earth, the colour is green: rich, deep and saturating.

The values of cool temperate rainforest are diverse. Its ancient origin enhances its scientific value, its uniqueness constitutes an important 'gene pool', a biological storehouse of genetic diversity. The forest is part of the tapestry of life forms on earth, which it is our responsibility to preserve. The mossy green boughs, the lush ferns and the cool air of the rainforest are of high recreational, aesthetic and (through sensitive development) economic value. Particularly in western Tasmania, the cool rainforests rank among the finest remaining forested wilderness areas in Australia.

Green and gold, Australia's colours.

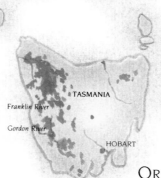

COOL TEMPERATE RAINFORESTS OF TASMANIA AND VICTORIA

Origins, Location, Distribution

In the state of Tasmania, an island separated from mainland Australia by Bass Strait since the last ice age, lies the remaining core-area of Australia's cool temperate rainforest. This forest type is very different from tropical, subtropical and warm temperate rainforests. It is derived from different ancestors, and the effect of cooler latitudes has also shaped its formation.

The origins of the forest date back many millennia. Scientists believe that about 200 million years ago the earth was divided into two major landmasses, Laurasia in the northern hemisphere and Gondwanaland in the south. As discussed elsewhere, about 120 million years ago this 'supercontinent' started to break up, the fledgling continents drifted apart and slowly (a few centimetres each year) moved towards their present positions.

Portions of the original Gondwanaland flora went with the drifting continents, and the ancient links between the flora of countries with a Gondwanaland ancestry can still be seen today, especially in countries inhabiting similar latitudes. It is not surprising that the present-day distribution of cool temperate rainforest is essentially confined to three regions: south-eastern Australia, the South Island of New Zealand and southern South America. Fossil evidence of similar forests has also been found in Antarctica.

In Australia in the period since Gondwanaland, rainforest has undergone both contractions and expansions. Around the time of the Gondwanaland breakup, myrtle beech or *Nothofagus*-dominated forest (ancestor of the present-day cool temperate rainforest) was distributed across the southern half of Australia. Then, with further northward drift of the continent and possibly some climatic change, the *Nothofagus* forest contracted to south-eastern Australia.

In the last million years or so, large fluctuations in sea level and climate have brought many changes in rainforest distribution. During ice ages the lowered sea level allowed *Nothofagus* forests to

Tree-trunks clothed in mosses and epiphytes

Eastern pigmy possum
(*Cercartetus nanus*).

spread northwards into highland regions. About 10 000 years ago cool temperate rainforest was widespread across south-eastern Australia and extended along the Great Dividing Range to the Queensland border.

Its present-day distribution is much more limited. It occurs in small isolated patches in New South Wales, generally in the higher coastal ranges and on the Barrington Tops. In Victoria, although nineteenth-century observers were very impressed with the luxuriance of extensive rainforests, of both cool temperate and warm temperate types, very little of these forests remain today. A recent estimate gives the total area as no more than 10 000 hectares.

There are four broad geographic regions containing rainforest communities in Victoria. The southern uplands of the Otway and Strzelecki ranges contain remnant sections of myrtle beech forests (*Nothofagus cunninghamii*) with the Otway communities being the most westerly occurrence of this forest type on the Australian continent. Similar forest types also occur in the Central Highlands to the north-east of Melbourne. The three communities – Otways, Strzeleckis and Central Highlands – have one thing in common: the major and catastrophic bushfires of 1939 which almost certainly limited the rainforest distribution. In many areas the rainforest is now emerging out of the unburnt areas into the surrounding eucalypt forest to reclaim its pre-1939 status.

The fourth area, East Gippsland, is undoubtedly the most interesting and diverse in the state and one of the most intriguing forested areas in Australia. Since early European settlement there has been considerable confusion about the status of East Gippsland rainforest types and this still exists today. Rainforests in the area have recently been classified into two distinct types: that of the lowland coastal region between Lakes Entrance and Mallacoota, where there is a frequent dominance of lilly pilly (*Acmena smithii*), has been classified as warm temperate rainforest; while the Coast Range rainforest to the north (Errinundra Plateau) is generally considered to be cool temperate.

The conservation importance of Victoria's rainforest has been consistently underestimated, particularly by governments. Their importance is strengthened by the fact that, compared to the more extensive rainforests of New South Wales, Queensland and Tasmania, Victorian rainforests are confined to small refugia in high-rainfall, sheltered locations. It is only in Tasmania that extensive areas of completely dominant cool temperate rainforest remain.

Most of Tasmania's rainforest is in the north-west of the state, where in the Savage and Sumac River areas there are large tracts of unbroken pure rainforest. Rainforest also occurs throughout the south-west and the central south, where, for example, the untouched valley of the Weld River is a rich mosaic of pure and mixed rainforest. Rainforest is also found throughout the uplands of the Cradle Mountain–Lake St Clair National Park, along the rivers in the Wild Rivers National Park and as scattered remnants in the highlands of the north-east, between Mt Maurice and Blue Tier. Tiny relict communities also occur in protected gullies and on south-facing slopes throughout the lowland east, in places such as the Douglas River and on the Tasman Peninsula.

Tasmania is Australia's most forested state. At the time of white settlement, forest covered about 80 per cent of the island. About 40 per cent cover now remains. Of this remaining forest, about 450 000 hectares or 13 per cent is pure rainforest. As will be discussed later, this figure is much larger if mixed rainforest (that with a eucalypt overstorey) is included.

Within Tasmania pure rainforest grows in regions with an annual rainfall of 1200 millimetres or more and with a monthly rainfall during summer of at least 40 millimetres. In a few areas with less rainfall (down to 800 millimetres each year and 25 millimetres monthly during summer) some rainforest development can also occur. Rainforest occurs on all soil types, from the infertile Pre-Cambrian quartzites to the nutrient-rich basalts.

Tasmanian devil (*Sacrophilus harrisii*) eating possum.

Fire is the main threat to its distribution; pure rainforest requires 300 to 400 fire-free years to develop. In Tasmania 47 per cent of the area that is climatically capable of supporting rainforest is buttongrass plains – the result of fires at much more frequent intervals.

Cool temperate rainforest in Tasmania is readily accessible; all the main roads in western Tasmania pass through rainforest. One particular area that has the added bonus of magnificent scenery is along the Lyell Highway. The highway crosses Tasmania east–west and passes through a number of areas of rainforest, including the beautiful communities of plants that line the banks of the Franklin River. It also provides (on the rare clear day – it is after all a *rainforest*) unparalleled views of the Western Tasmanian World Heritage area.

Probably the most accessible stands of rainforest in Victoria occur in the Otways along Youngs Creek in the Aire River Valley, and the Mait's Rest Reserve in the Parker River Valley.

FOREST STRUCTURE

High rainfall, high temperature and sunshine are the ingredients for producing the richest forests. There are many areas on earth with enough rainfall and sunshine, but only in the tropics are the temper-

Franklin River, Frenchman's Cap National Park.

mania with up to 95 per cent rainforest canopy component (called mixed forest, not mixed *rain*forest, by the Commission) are managed in essentially the same way as those with no rainforest component. Such management is causing a major reduction in the rainforest component of Tasmania's forests. The debate over what constitutes a rainforest community is similarly vigorous in Victoria where eucalypt emergents are found in communities of rainforest species.

Cool temperate rainforest in Tasmania can be categorised into four broad subgroups: callidendrous, thamnic, implicate, and open montane rainforests.

CALLIDENDROUS RAINFOREST typifies the popular idea of a cool rainforest. The name is derived from the Greek words *kalos* (beautiful) and *dendron* (tree). Myrtles form a tall protective canopy, under which the air is cool and moist. It is open and delightful walking on age-old accumulations of leaf and twig, between tree ferns and the scalloped trunks of the myrtles. Groves of sassafras, tall and graceful, often have their branches hung with long moss and lichen.

THAMNIC RAINFOREST (from the Greek *thamnos* meaning 'shrub') is intermediate between the tall callidendrous forests and the low tangled implicate communities. There is greater diversity of tree species; as well as myrtle, there may be Huon, celery top or King Billy pine, leatherwood and sassafras. Shrubs are common, such as the broad-leaved native laurel and the long-stemmed 'triffid-impersonating' pandani. The leech fern is aptly named and abundant. In late summer the pink climbing heath is in flower with a mass of pendulous pink and red bells.

IMPLICATE RAINFORESTS (from the Latin adjective *implicatus*, meaning 'tangled' or 'interwoven'). In defining this forest, Jarman and her co-authors in *Rainforest in Tasmania* (1984) state that this refers to: 'the dense network of stems in the understorey which makes upright movement through these forests almost impossible ... The understorey is continuous with the canopy.' It must surely have been such a forest that Osbourne Geeves saw on his exploratory trip in 1881 to the headwaters of the Old River in the south-west: '... grass trees from knee high to 30 feet, mingled with horizontal scrub and occasional cutting grass ... [We] took an hour to clear a place big enough to pitch our tent, and another to collect firewood and bedding. Long before we had firewood it began, as I had suspected, to rain ... started off after breakfast ... through scrub, moss, prickles of scrub, tea-tree ... heavy black clouds overhead ... so dark I could scarcely read the points of the compass with my spectacles ...' All this makes quite understandable the apology by Jarman and her co-authors that

Mt Bobs moss forest, Tasmania.

The variably coloured leaves of the beech tree *Nothofagus gunnii*.

Cool temperate rainforest with *Notofagus* beech, Cradle Valley, Tasmania.

'detailed definition of individual plant communities within implicate rainforest has proved difficult . . .'!

OPEN MONTANE RAINFOREST is restricted to high-altitude situations, principally amongst boulder fields or outcropping rocks, or along streams. These are the pencil pine forests of the central and south-west highlands. The understorey is sometimes thick and always distinct; often the very beautiful association with the deciduous beech occurs.

Yellow flatworm with mosses, fungi and fern fronds, Tasmania.

Unlike eucalypt forests, rainforests evolved in an environment with a low fire frequency, and consequently all rainforest species are fire sensitive. Because of the cool moist microclimate beneath the closed canopy, pure rainforest is highly resistant to burning, and fires often extinguish at the rainforest edge. However, disturbance of the canopy increases the threat of fire, by drying the understorey and promoting the invasion of flammable species such as eucalypts. When rainforest does burn it can do so very fiercely, and recovery afterwards is slow because of the relatively slow growth rate of rainforest species. In addition, burnt rainforest is highly susceptible to subsequent fires. Successive fires that destroy the rainforest trees before they reach seed-bearing age will eliminate these species.

Where pure rainforest has been disturbed by fire, mixed forest is the usual result: rainforest species growing beneath eucalypt emergents. The rainforest species will shade out any further eucalypt seedlings which require full sunlight to grow. If the 350-year lifespan of the overstorey eucalypts is survived free of fire, pure rainforest again results.

FLORA

Myrtle is the most abundant and widespread of all cool temperate rainforest trees. It has a lifespan of about 350 years. Though its leaves are small, they are very numerous and form a dense canopy in pure stands. Very little light penetrates this canopy, and the forest floor is often reduced to a surface cover of ferns, mosses and lichens.

The most common tree association with myrtle is sassafras (*Atherosperma moschatum*), although blackwood (*Acacia melanoxylon*) can also occur. In Tasmania endemic species that may be present include leatherwood (*Eucryphia lucida*), horizontal (*Anodopetalum biglandulosum*), and such conifers as Huon pine (*Lagarostrobus franklinii*), celery top pine (*Phyllocladus aspleniifolius*) and King Billy and pencil pines (*Athrotaxis selaginoides* and *A. cupressoides*).

In Victoria, a higher proportion of remaining rainforest is mixed or transitional forest with eucalypt emergents (eucalypt trees that emerge above the rainforest canopy). Perhaps representing some as yet untold story of biogeographical history both the Otways and East Gippsland rainforests contain different major components. The Otways, dominated by magnificent specimens of myrtle beech, do not contain any sassafras. Interestingly, by contrast, the East Gippsland rainforests do not contain any beech but sassafras is a major component.

The softwood pines of Tasmania form a link with the ancient conifer forests that existed before the division of Gondwanaland. Individual trees can grow to a great age. Huon pine in particular is one of the oldest living organisms on earth. Trees 2100 years old have been found, and it is widely thought that members of the species can live for more than 3000 years. Trees alive today were growing before the time of Christ and have lived through the rise and fall of many civilisations. The timber cut from Huon pine is also extraordinarily resistant to rot and decay, hence its world-famous reputation as a boat-building timber. Buried Huon pine logs, still intact, have been carbon dated at more than 6000 years of age.

Members of the genus *Athrotaxis*, which includes King Billy and pencil pines, are also long lived. Ages in excess of 1000 years have been recorded. These trees belong to the same family as the Californian redwoods and are the only representatives of this family in the southern hemisphere.

The celery top pine is something of a botanical curiosity in that it appears to fall somewhere between conifers and flowering plants on the evolutionary scale. Leaves are present at the seedling stage, but are replaced by flattened green branchlets in the mature tree. These structures resemble the lobes of a celery leaf, hence the name.

The cool temperate rainforests are entirely evergreen, with one Tasmanian exception: the deciduous beech (*Nothofagus gunnii*). This, one of Australia's few native winter-deciduous trees, produces a stunning display of red, gold and vivid orange amidst frosted highland tarns and magnificent mountain backdrops.

Thick mosses carpet roots and forest floor.

The understorey layer of plants in cool temperate rainforests can vary from simply not occurring to being contiguous with the canopy, though, like the overstorey there are usually few higher plant species in it. The most variety occurs within the lower plant forms. Ferns are common and of diverse type. Lichens, mosses and fungi are abundant, brightly coloured and in a multitude of shapes and sizes. But lianes and scrambling plants are rare, and parasitic and carnivorous vascular plants are entirely absent.

Most trees grow with single-stem trunks, although there are notable exceptions to this, in particular the infamous 'horizontal' that grows as a chaotic tumble of intertwining branches. This happens as slender stems bend and lean, then form new growth along their length. These new stems also bend, new shoots grow upwards, and the process continues. To travel in such country is a painstaking gymnastic exercise of climb and squeeze, frequently at an alarming height above firm ground.

Buttresses are rare in cool forests, unlike their northern counterparts, although 'finger-cages' may form. These occur when seedlings of the sassafras tree establish themselves on large decaying logs and send roots downwards to the soil. In time, the logs break down and each sassafras tree is supported on a sturdy web of fingerlike roots.

The forests of East Gippsland are the most spectacular of the cool temperate rainforests of Victoria even though the largest single area is only an estimated 150 hectares. The forests are renowned for their unusual associations, particularly the intermingling of huge eucalypts with rainforest species and the unusual sizes that many species attain.

On the Errinundra Plateau, an outstanding mountain refuge, the mountain tea-tree (*Leptospermum grandifolium*) attains heights of 25 metres while other common species – sassafras, blackwood, privet, mock-olive, forest geebung and tree lomatia – also grow to sizes unknown or unusual elsewhere.

The waratah (*Telopea truncata*) in flower.

Perhaps the most fascinating example of this is the mountain plum pine (*Podocarpus lawrencii*) which on Errinundra Plateau grows into a large tree, usually of 7–10 metres but claimed to attain up to 17 metres in some cases. Elsewhere in the Victorian high country it grows only as a dwarf sprawling shrub. It is felt likely that, on further investigation, it will gain separate species status.

Another feature of great beauty is the spring display of the bright red Gippsland waratah (*Telopea oreades*). Its brilliant splashes of colour scattered throughout the forest delight the botanist and nature lover alike.

The ridges near the edge of Errinundra Plateau provide a true understanding of the complex associations, and hence the conservation significance, of East Gippsland. Rainforest communities of sassafras, black olive-berry, blackwood and mountain plum pine overlap with giant eucalypt forest communities of shining gum, brown barrel, mountain ash, (its easternmost occurrence in Australia), mountain grey gum and many others.

The warm temperate rainforest pockets of Victoria occur only in South Gippsland and the lowland areas of East Gippsland. They are most easily characterised by the presence of lilly pilly (*Acmena smithii*) and a much greater number of lianes. Locally the forest is called 'jungle'. However, despite its affinities with northern rainforests, it is distinctly a temperate form.

A typically moss- and fern-dominated cool temperate rainforest understorey.

The forests around Mallacoota contain some of the most botanically confusing plant associations in the state. Rainforest status changes from cool to warm temperate from one gully to the next and in some cases there is a hint of subtropical status, especially in the Howe Range north of Mallacoota. All of Victoria's five epiphytic orchids grow in the rainforests around Mallacoota, with orange blossom and giant rock orchids reaching their southernmost range within kilometres of the border town.

In the south, near Orbost, a strange outlying community of cabbage palm can be found along Cabbage Tree Creek. The nearest community is found 300 kilometres away in New South Wales.

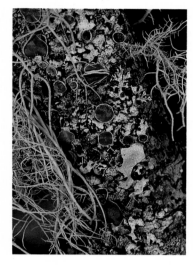

Various lichens and the circular reproductive fruiting bodies of one species.

FAUNA

Compared with other forest types, few animals live in the cool temperate rainforest. When you visit a rainforest, large animals in particular are notably absent. However, cockatoos, black or sulphur-crested, may be noisily conspicuous along valleys and amidst a high forest canopy. Small quick birds that are difficult to identify may flit through low undergrowth, or a thrush may run startled from your approach. Large mammals are seldom seen, although the soft leaf-litter rustling of a small native mouse might be heard on a quiet evening. Ground-dwelling invertebrates will be found if you look, inhabiting fallen vegetation and in the open spaces along rivers and rock outcrops. Insects and spiders, including ferocious mosquitoes, can be abundant in the warm season.

Tasmania's fauna, like its flora, consists of at least two elements: firstly, archaic forms that have affinities with other fragments of the ancient Gondwanaland supercontinent; and secondly, forms whose affinities lie with the fauna of mainland Australia and the lands to the north in south-east Asia. Although Tasmania's fauna is depauperate, in general, compared with mainland Australia, there are many animals in the first category described above that are either endemic to the island (are found nowhere else) or have their stronghold here. The long isolation of Tasmania from the mainland between ice ages and the consequent lack of competition with other species have allowed the survival of many of these forms.

Twenty-five mammal species have been recorded in Tasmanian rainforests, which represents about two-thirds of the state's total mammal fauna. However, of those, 14 are either transients or occasional visitors making use of rainforest edges, sites along rivers or areas disturbed by fire. Of the remainder, none is confined to rainforest habitats. Apart from the long-tailed mouse (*Pseudomys higgin-*

Tree ferns and mosses at Errinundra Plateau, eastern Victoria.

The star fungus (*Aseroe rubra*) attracts flies to its reproductive spores for dispersal.

sii), none occurs primarily in rainforest. This absence of rainforest fauna is paralleled in the *Nothofagus*-dominated forests of South America.

Unlike many other Tasmanian forest habitats, cool temperate rainforest is notable for its lack of introduced mammal species. Only the house mouse (*Mus musculus*) and the feral cat (*Felis catus*) have been recorded in undisturbed rainforest.

Because of the lack of vegetation at ground level, terrestrial herbivores are poorly represented. Only the rufous wallaby or Tasmanian pademelon (*Thylogale billardierii*) is commonly found, although the wombat and Bennett's wallaby occur on the edges of cool temperate rainforest. Carnivores are not abundant, probably because of low prey densities, and those that do occur range over wide areas. Rodents are the most numerically abundant mammals, feeding on both plant and insect material.

Twenty-one bird species regularly inhabit cool temperate rainforest, in addition to a number of occasional and vagrant visitors. No bird species is restricted to rainforest, and no threatened or endangered birds occur in it. There are several introduced species such as the superb lyrebird and the blackbird; however, their invasion rates are slow and neither yet inhabits remote rainforests.

Six birds of prey use rainforest regularly. These include the wedge-tailed eagle (*Aquila audax*), the white-breasted sea eagle (*Haliaeetus leucogaster*), the masked owl (*Tyto novaehollandiae*) and the grey goshawk (*Accipiter novaehollandiae*). The male grey goshawk is sufficiently agile to hunt like a sparrow hawk, but the female, nearly twice the size of the male, is powerful enough to hunt like an eagle, taking large preys such as herons and currawongs. The masked owl is the only owl associated with rainforest.

Information on reptiles is sparse, although it is apparent that no more than six species can live in cool temperate rainforest, and none of these is confined to this type of forest. As with all reptiles, sunlight is essential to warm the blood up to operating temperature. Within the closed canopy of the rainforest this becomes difficult. The most successful species such as skinks (*Leiolopisma metallica*) have adopted an arboreal habitat, thus increasing their range of basking sites for temperature regulation. Others such as the tiger snake (*Notechis ater*) are semi-aquatic and exploit the more open forest canopy along the watercourses. None of the reptile species known in cool temperate rainforest in Tasmania is endangered.

As with reptiles, what we know about frogs of the forest is limited. Four species are known to occur; none is thought to be endangered.

The general state of knowledge on invertebrates is again poor.

With the exception of the Dermaptera (a small mixed group that includes earwigs), which are absent, there are few, if any, major absences or overrepresentations of the major invertebrates in Tasmanian rainforest. In contrast to the eucalypt forests, there appear to be few defoliating insects feeding on rainforest trees. The kinds of invertebrate found in particular habitat types are not consistent across Tasmania, so the insects that inhabit, for example, a sassafras grove of the north-east highlands, will not necessarily be the same as those in a similar forest type in the south-west. Unlike the higher animals, the invertebrates of Tasmanian rainforests appear to be more regionally divided.

Generally, the cool temperate rainforest of Tasmania contains fewer animal species than comparable wet sclerophyll forest, and none is known to be endangered. However, many of the animals that do have a close association with rainforests are endemic (found only in Tasmania) and are often derived from Gondwanaland ancestors.

Many of the generalisations made of Tasmanian rainforest fauna also apply to Victoria. It is thought that no vertebrate species is completely dependent on Victorian rainforest habitat. However, there are various rare and endangered species that are closely associated with this forest type and would almost certainly suffer further from its destruction or degradation. These include the Tasmanian pipistrelli (a bat) and the spotted tree frog (*Litoria maculata*). Other important species associated with the rainforest and rainforest–eucalypt associations are the tiger-quoll – the only remaining species of the three quolls once found in Victoria – the powerful owl, sooty owl, black-eyed flycatcher and Lewin's honeyeater.

The crozier, or new frond, of a fern unfurls.

HISTORY OF HUMAN USE

In Tasmania the logging of Huon and King Billy pines was the first major industry to utilise rainforest timbers. The Huon pine, in particular, was highly prized especially for boat building. One of the reasons for establishing a convict settlement at Macquarie Harbour in 1822 was to provide a labour force to harvest pines from the remote and wild western rivers, the Gordon, Franklin and Denison.

After the convict days, 'piners' worked for decades along the river under gruelling conditions of rugged terrain, dense vegetation, fierce storms and flooding. Cut logs were branded, then floated downstream to mills. However, pirating was common; less scrupulous men downstream would intercept the logs, cut off the initial brand and replace it with their own. The range of uses for King Billy pine timber included boat building, joinery, railway sleepers and roof shingles.

An epiphytic *Pyrrosia* fern exhibits its reproductive spores.

A myrtle beech (*Nothofagus cunninghamii*) covered in epiphytic ferns.

After the early piners, there were three distinct phases in the use of Tasmania's rainforests by white Tasmanians. The first phase lasted from 1830 to 1930 and involved the wholesale clearance of large areas of rainforest to meet the demands of settlement and agriculture. In the north-west coast area, in particular, extensive stands of fine timber were found on rich, red, arable soils. Clearing of these forests formed the basis of a timber trade, and by the late 1850s timber tramways had penetrated 15 kilometres inland from the coast. The period 1850–70 has been described as one of 'great expectations', abounding with reports of the great wealth to be obtained from the forests. These reports were propagated and used by businessmen as a means of securing government finance for access tramways. It was said that the prosperity of the colony would increase as a result, for farmers would follow the timbergetters. In part, this prediction came true, as the more fertile areas of the north-west are today some of the best farming land in Tasmania. However, not all forests cleared from the region were on fertile soils.

After World War One, motor transport enabled the establishment of sawmills in the backhills, and competition for the remaining areas of timber on less fertile ground often approached open warfare. Of this period Scott wrote in 1963: 'In the past forestry was regarded as secondary to agriculture, a source of revenue to help meet the costs of clearing the land for farming. Under such circumstances, even land above 500 metres, having a rainfall of greater than 1500 mm was wholly cleared; it proved to be of very poor quality for farming and was later abandoned. Such land, which occurs extensively in the northwest and northeast, is now a rabbit infested wilderness of bracken, blackberries, shrubs and dead logs.'

Raindrops sparkle on a freshly fallen bloom.

Simultaneous with the clearing of rainforest for agriculture was the squandering of huge volumes of rainforest woods in the mining belt surrounding Queenstown. Here, cutting for fuel for the mining furnaces, along with fire and air pollution, changed the lush King Billy pine rainforest into today's ecological desert of bare eroded hills.

In the second phase, between 1938 and 1963, three major pulp and paper companies commenced operations in Tasmania. The companies were granted exclusive and long-term rights to the pulpwood (trees that could not be used by the sawlogging industry) over large areas of the state's publicly owned forests. The major vegetation type used by the companies was young eucalypt species, thus the focus of both the companies and the state Forestry Commission was and is today the promotion of preferred ages and types of eucalypt forest and the suppression of other vegetation types that restrict the growth of eucalypts – in particular, rainforest species.

The results of forest management practices to achieve these ends, particularly the practice of clearfelling and burning forests on short rotation times (40–120 years), are now becoming apparent. When the 300–400 years necessary for eucalypt forest with a rainforest understorey to become rainforest is shortened to the rotation times practised by the Forestry Commission, the forests are artificially held in the young eucalypt stage of development. They will never become rainforest. Further, the constant clearing and burning at short time intervals eliminates many of the more fire-sensitive rainforest elements from the understorey. This, coupled with the fact that only the commercial eucalypt species are resown, means that the 'forest' that results will be little more than even-aged stands of eucalypt species with a depauperate, fire-tolerant understorey. Thus the major effect of the pulp companies has not been directly on pure rainforest but on the potential 'transitional' forest that could become rainforest if natural processes were allowed to operate.

The third phase began in 1971 with the advent of the export woodchipping industry. This industry, like the earlier pulpwood industry, was allowed to take wood from large areas of state forest to convert into woodchips. The most distinguishing feature of the third phase is the vast increase in the scale of timbercutting operations. In the decade since 1971 the amount of timber cut for pulpwood has increased by nearly 500 per cent, almost entirely due to the commencement of the export woodchipping industry. The direct effect of this has been to greatly increase the amount of forest undergoing the changes outlined in phase two. The indirect effect has been to cause the Forestry Commission to examine the possibility of logging pure rainforest. This will be looked at further in the section dealing with conservation status.

Trunks of the shining gum (*Eucalyptus nitens*), East Gippsland, Victoria.

As well as being harvested for pulp, rainforest woods are beginning to be used for ends more appropriate to their qualities. Huon pine and blackwood have for years been highly sought after by the craft and furniture industries. And in the past decade, species such as leatherwood, sassafras, horizontal, myrtle, and the other native pines have also become increasingly popular for craft and furniture items of fine design. The beautiful white-blossomed leatherwood is also the basis for the leatherwood honey industry, for many years a major export industry for Tasmania.

Most rainforest destruction in Victoria has occurred during agricultural clearing. *Nothofagus* gully forests have disappeared in many areas of the Otway and Strzelecki Ranges as a direct result of clearing for dairy farming and potato growing. In both these cases large areas of cleared land were found to be unproductive and were

Pink fungal fruits, fallen flowers, leaves and branches are but some leaf-litter constituents.

A sparse canopy is advantageous to the tree ferns at Errinundra Plateau, eastern Victoria.

A thaw exposes the forest-floor plants and litter.

subsequently used for some of the first exotic forest plantations in Australia. The Aire Valley plantation in the Otways is about 7000 hectares while most of the eastern Strzelecki Range is now planted to pine. Small pockets of *Nothofagus* rainforest remain with only about 300 hectares protected within national or state park boundaries.

The situation in the *Nothofagus* forests of the Central Highlands is only marginally better. This is partly because most rainforests in the highlands are inaccessible for agricultural use. However forestry operations and fire have severely degraded many existing stands of *Nothofagus* and the major remaining healthy stands are found predominantly in the more remote regions on the south side of the Great Divide.

Loss of lowland temperate rainforest in East Gippsland is difficult to quantify. Many areas of coastal rainforest disappeared under pressure from agriculture well before their existence was recorded. As will be discussed in the Conversation Status section, continued attrition of Victoria's limited rainforests is occurring principally as a result of logging operations.

CONSERVATION STATUS

Two factors have aided the survival of the relatively large areas of cool temperate rainforest that remain in Tasmania today. Firstly, inaccessability: the vast bulk of the rainforest lies in the west of the state. This area catches the brunt of the rains driven by the Roaring Forties, it is a wild wet wilderness, and even now there is little settlement in the region. Only the lure of mineral wealth (such as at Queenstown) or the prospect of the valuable pines has tempted people to live voluntarily in the region for long periods.

Secondly, and probably most importantly, little of economic worth apart from the native pines and blackwood has so far been found in the rainforests. In consequence, most of the present-day impact on pure rainforest has been indirect or incidental, the result of fire, the opening of the canopy for roading or inundation for hydro-electricity. However, with the probable use of pure rainforest for forestry purposes after 1988, the future for the cool temperate rainforests of Tasmania is in doubt.

All of the major threats to cool temperate rainforest come directly from, or are greatly aggravated by, human activities. Thus the fundamental and underlying threat to rainforest is in the low worth given to it by our society. This mentality stems from the perception of the early colonisers, who saw the land, and in particular rainforest, as desolate, damp, forbidding 'scrub'. In Victoria, also, rainforest has been colloquially known as 'jungle'.

Since white settlement, at least a third of Tasmania's rainforest and more than half of the transitional or mixed forest rich in rainforest species have been cleared.

The primary direct threats to cool temperate rainforest are fire, forestry, hydro-electric schemes (in Tasmania), mining, water pollution, clearing for agriculture, and uncontrolled recreational activities. Then there is incidental damage from the introduction of disease, feral animals, exotic weeds and from erosion.

Fire is the greatest single threat to rainforest. Today, 95 per cent of all fires in Tasmania are human caused. Vast areas of rainforest have been burnt by successive wildfires. In the past two decades 15 per cent of Tasmanian rainforest has been burnt, frequently reducing them in area and downgrading them to eucalypt forest and buttongrass plains. Paradoxically these fires, often lit to try to decrease the risk of wildfire, change the rainforest composition towards more flammable communities which make the likelihood of future fires much greater. Some rainforest communities, principally the slow-growing conifers, once burnt are lost forever. If present trends continue, mature stands of trees such as pencil, King Billy and Huon pine will be eliminated.

Cool temperate rainforest microhabitats: a pool, mosses and tree-fern trunks.

Threats to pure rainforest from forestry are the most serious in the long term. Seventy-nine per cent of Tasmania's rainforest lies on Crown land or in state forest and will therefore be available for logging in the future. Although state-owned pure rainforest is protected by moratorium from logging until 1988, no such restrictions apply to private land, and rainforests in north-west Tasmania are presently being clearfelled for eucalypt and pine plantations. The Forestry Commission in Tasmania has given every indication that there will be moves to log pure rainforest on public land after 1988. This will be partly to use the rainforest woods for pulp but more importantly to convert the land to the more economically productive eucalypt plantations.

In the wet forests of Tasmania and Victoria, there is extensive clearfelling of 'mixed' forests and subsequent regeneration to eucalypts. As was pointed out in the section on human use, this is effectively destroying potential rainforest. If these transitional, potential rainforests are included in an assessment of the area of rainforest in Tasmania, the figure more than doubles, from 450 000 to 976 000 hectares.

Much rainforest has been inundated behind hydro-electric dams. If the Lower Gordon scheme (the one that would have flooded the Franklin and Lower Gordon Rivers) had proceeded, 45 per cent of Tasmania's riverine rainforest, the sole habitat of Huon pine, would have been lost over a period of just 20 years. Already, 16 per cent has been inundated through existing schemes.

Myrtle wilt is a fungal disease which kills trees after they have been attacked by a small beetle, called the platypus beetle. In recent years it has become more widespread in Tasmanian forests, its impact being greatly increased through human disturbances such as roading. Fortunately the introduced root rot fungus, *Phytophthora cinnamomi*, is restricted by the low soil temperatures under the canopy of cool temperate rainforest. However, the fungus does produce fire-resistant spores which can kill regenerating forest species in the more structurally open forest that follows a fire.

Water pollution is a largely uncontrolled problem in western Tasmania; it can seriously affect floodbank rainforest communities. Huon pines on the lower Savage River were devastated when a tailings dam failed and the resultant sludge was deposited along the riverbanks, killing all plant life there.

The Forests Department has estimated that there are presently 13 270 hectares of rainforest in Victoria. This figure includes warm and cool temperate rainforest types and does not include emergent associations. The Victorian Forests Department does not accept that emergent associations are rainforest — despite the fact that many scientists hold a contrary view. The Errinundra sassafras–shining gum association, an excellent example of permanent emergent associations is, as a result, being logged out. Conservation of cool temperate rainforest is poor, with only 8 per cent reserved, while conservation status of warm temperate types is only marginally better, with 25 per cent of the existing 3400 hectares reserved.

In Victoria there is poor correlation between national park boundaries and rainforests although a large national park on Errinundra Plateau would begin to solve this problem. Most southern, central and eastern parks contain small sections of rainforest with Croajingolong, Drummer and Alfred National Parks containing the most significant stands of warm temperate associations. Unfortunately many of these stands were drastically altered by a recent bushfire. Other national parks contain mostly *Nothofagus* associations, the best being in Otway, Tarra Valley, Baw Baw and Wonangatta–Moroka National Parks. All other reserves are state forest reserves which cannot be considered permanent under present legislation.

There are *no* national parks in the Errinundra–Rodger River– Bowen Range area although the present Labor Government (1985) has promised a large national park in this region. The region contains one of the few remaining large virgin forest areas in Australia. It extends from the west side of Errinundra Plateau over the Rodger

A miniature fungus fruit erupts from the mosses.

A crowded forest floor at Errinundra Plateau.

A magnificent emergent shining gum (*Eucalyptus nitens*).

River and Bowen Range. This region has never been logged and is all that Victoria has to offer as a true forest wilderness. Unfortunately logging operations are threatening to engulf this magnificent forest.

At present in Tasmania, only about 9 per cent of rainforest is protected in state reserves. These reserves are regionally biased. In the north-west of the state, where most of the rainforest occurs, there is no reserve (of any kind) that is large enough to be ecologically viable. Furthermore, of the 34 cool temperate rainforest communities that occur in Tasmania, exactly half are either entirely absent or inadequately represented in existing reserves. These include open forests of pencil pines, such as are found at Mt Pillinger, outside of the boundary of Cradle Mountain National Park; the implicate myrtle–scoparia rainforest with King Billy pine, found on the north-east ridge of Mt Anne; the open high-altitude forests which occur along the Great Western Tiers; and a number of Huon pine community types.

As discussed, Victorian rainforests, particularly those of East Gippsland, are unusual mainly due to the close association of rainforest (closed forest) species and eucalypt species. In most areas the tallest and best commercial timbers, like mountain ash and brown barrel, grow within or in close proximity to rainforests. In many cases rainforests are considered to be 'emergent', and would therefore become the dominant forest type in gullies after the eucalypt species mature; i.e. rainforest is the climax association. In other areas rainforest and eucalypt species occur in multi-aged stands and coexist quite naturally.

However, these close associations have created enormous management problems. Eucalypts are the only commercially extracted timber in Victoria and, because fire is used for regeneration of this genus, rainforests are managed so as to contain rainforest species or remove them from commercial forest areas. Rainforests are also damaged where buffer areas are logged, roaded, burnt or clearfelled. All activity adds to disturbance and to weed and fire penetration. Breaks in the canopy can encourage dieback of rainforest species. It is obvious, then, that reservation of large areas of naturally occuring eucalypt–rainforest associations is crucial if rainforest communities are to survive in Victoria.

A decaying shining gum (*Eucalyptus nitens*).

Tasmanian pademelon (Thylogale billardierii)

8
DRY RAINFORESTS AND OTHER UNIQUE RAINFORESTS

DR A.N. GILLISON

THE WORD 'rainforest' conjures up images of tall tropical closed forests or jungles whose leafy mantles enclose a bewildering variety of growth forms, all restricted to regions of high rainfall and high temperatures. It comes as a surprise to many people when they are introduced to certain Australian 'rainforests', for these may be anything but the stereotyped image. Among them are the so-called 'monsoon forests' and 'dry' scrubs or vine thickets which occur not in the continually moist environments but in regions with pronounced wet and dry seasons. The aim of this chapter is to introduce a range of rainforest habitats that go beyond the usual image of rainforest, but which are just as biologically exciting and have their own special aesthetic appeal.

The main reason why 'dry' rainforests are still rainforests despite their difference from the taller, wetter and better-known forests, is that they also have a closed canopy, and many plant genera are common to both. The monsoon forests (Chapter 3) contain the taller 'dry' rainforests, so in this chapter we shall consider mainly the drier end of the seasonal spectrum that supports the lower thickets and vine scrubs. The fascinating phenomena of rainforests growing on sand – coastal or littoral rainforests – are also considered briefly.

As mentioned in Chapter 1, rainforests in Australia today represent the product of a great series of environmental changes which have acted as an evolutionary sieve. For general purposes, therefore,

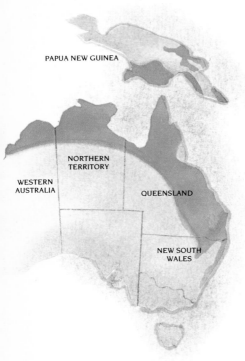

Shaded area indicates the potential bioclimate for 'dry' seasonal rainforests on the continental joint land mass of Australia and island of New Guinea: hotter areas in the north, cooler and less seasonal areas in the south-east corner.

Dry rainforest thicket, Alligator River area, Northern Territory.

it is convenient to regard the present distribution of rainforests as derived from an ancient palaeotropic stock of Gondwanan affinity — which for only a relatively brief period has been modified by white people and, before them, by Aboriginal people for at least 40 000 years. The Aborigines, who fired the landscape for hunting and other purposes, indirectly controlled the spatial limits of rainforests.

All these influences have provided a range of environmental gradients, comprising a great variety of savannas, woodlands and forests. Because of the profound influence of climate, it is not surprising that Australian rainforests have been described in terms of four main floristic/geographic elements: the 'hot dry' in the north, the 'hot moist' in the north-east, and the 'warm dry' and 'cool moist' in the south-east. This chapter deals mostly with the 'hot dry' and the 'warm dry', both experiencing a distinctly seasonal climate, with seasonality diminishing towards the cooler margins of the 'warm dry' region. It is within the wetter extremes of the 'hot dry' zone that the well-known and structurally well-formed 'monsoon' Indo-Malesian forests are distributed. (These are more fully described in Chapter 3).

Within the general 'monsoon' category there is an approximate division into deciduous vine forest or deciduous vine thickets that exist mainly on relatively nutrient-rich soils of basaltic origin or calcareous beach sands or levee systems associated with seasonal inundation. Poorer and more skeletal soils support vegetation with a greater proportion of small-leaved evergreen species; and the plants tend to be more closely related to the rainforests of the wetter and less-seasonal east coast of the continent. It has been argued that the 'hot dry' forests are species-poor, but this is not necessarily true of some of the better-formed seasonal forests and thickets in eastern Australia, especially those on the richer soils.

In general, the 'hot dry' rainforests include the 'softwood scrubs' or the 'bottle-tree scrubs' and semi-evergreen vine thickets which at the turn of the century probably covered about 7 million hectares in inland parts of Queensland and New South Wales. Associated with these scrubs or thickets are unique Australian elements such as brigalow (Acacia harpopylla) and some of the more Gondwanan gymnosperms such as hoop pine (Araucaria cunninghamii) and cypress pine (Callitris columellaris). Unlike the moister rainforests of Australia, the dry rainforests are not only extremely variable in species and structure but also difficult to show at any but the larger map scales because of their fragmentary distribution. As their potential distribution is at present limited by seasonal firing and clearing for agriculture, the map indicates the bioclimatically determined potential area that could be covered by this vegetation type.

1 Wet-season aspect of softwood scrub, central Queensland.

2 Brigalow softwood scrub, central Queensland.

3 Softwood scrub, 'Forty Mile Scrub', North Queensland.

King parrot in bunya pine.

The characteristic shape of the bunya pine.

Airborne seeds glow in the setting sun against silhouetted bunya pines.

Christmas orchid, Fraser Island.

(up to 1400 millimetres annual rainfall, with less than 50 millimetres per month in winter) is reflected in the winter-deciduous red cedar (*Toona australis*), white cedar (*Melia azedarach*), batwing coral tree (*Erythrina vespertilio*), the ash (*Flindersia macrophylla*) and occasionally the deciduous fig (*Ficus superba* var. *henniana*). Other floristic alliances may be characterised by brown myrtle (*Choricarpia leptopetala*) and shatterwood (*Backhousia sciadophora*).

Watercourses in dry rainforest areas of northern New South Wales and southern Queensland are commonly occupied by black bean (*Castanospermum australe*), silky oak (*Grevillea robusta*) and *Waterhousea floribunda*. In northern New South Wales, some of the hoop pine-dominated thickets and coastal scrubs are well represented in the Byron Bay area, where many thicket species that are common in the warmer north grow less densely.

RAINFORESTS ON COASTAL SANDS

The littoral environment, often with its low-nutrient sands, is perhaps where one would least expect to find rainforest. Yet in Australia, some of the most outstanding examples of well-structured rainforest are to be found on the littoral formations, especially along the northern and eastern coasts of Australia. These comprise the dune thicket formations already described in northern Australia; and related, mostly evergreen, well-formed (and mostly fire-protected) rainforests on deep Pleistocene coastal dune sands in southern Queensland at Cooloola National Park and on the nearshore sand islands (Fraser, Moreton and Stradbroke), and in northern New South Wales at Iluka. These are sometimes described as evergreen notophyll forests or vine forests and usually include a high proportion of hard-leaved or 'sclerophyllous' rainforest trees.

Although the sands on which they grow are very low in nutrients, the existence of the forests is usually due to the availability of water at depth and to the presumed capacity of the plants to accumulate nutrients from the atmosphere and to recycle them via highly specialised fungi or mycorrhizae in the well-formed litter layer and upper root zone. The very beautiful and well-developed rainforests of Fraser Island, the world's largest pure sand island, have been a source of timber supply for some time, but it is known from experience in logging rainforests on sands in other parts of the world (for example the northern Amazon) that recovery is extremely slow. It seems unfortunate that more effort is not being made to find an alternative to logging these fascinating forests.

Lush subtropical rainforest on Fraser Island.

Turpentine forest (*Syncarpia glomulifera*).

Vine thicket along freshwater creek, Fraser Island.

Bangalow palm forest, Fraser Island.

Huge paperbark trees near the mouth of the Johnstone River
bear the brunt of tropical storms and act as a buffer for the rainforest behind.

250

Behind the shelter of the paperbarks the rainforest struggles to establish itself.

A crab shelters in a hollow mangrove log on Hinchinbrook Island.

Because of the low nutrients in sandy ecosystems, most of the leaves tend to be small (microphyll and notophyll) and evergreen and in this way similar to those of plant communities of the inland evergreen vine thickets. Both palms and gymnosperms are characteristic of rainforests on sand, and there are often intervening communities or mixtures of eucalypts, wattles and tea-trees.

In Cooloola, on Pleistocene dune formations, the stately, straight, kauri pine (*Agathis robusta*, a close relative of *Araucaria*) occurs together with hoop pine and brown pine (*Podocarpus elatus*) in association with an extensive palm community of piccabeen palms (*Archontophoenix cunninghamiana*) and many other rainforest tree species.

In the understorey, the tree-heaths *Trochocarpa laurina* and *Alyxia ruscifolia*, together with the cycad *Macrozamia miquelii* also suggest a continuum with other low-nutrient ecosystems away from the sands, while bolwarra (*Eupomatia laurina*) indicates connections with cooler 'lauraceous' forest types. The smaller tree genera such as *Canthium*, *Clerodendrum*, *Denhamia* and *Drypetes*, have floristic and structural affinities with the inland thickets, while *Canarium australasicum* and *Ficus platypoda* and *F. watkinsiana*, and vines such as *Hoya australis* and *Marsdenia* spp. show relationships with the more deciduous rainforests of the drier and more seasonal north. On the forest edges, the cypress (*Callitris columellaris*) and the she-oak (*Casuarina littoralis*) with rather similar foliage, are common as in areas in the seasonal north. Many of the species listed above also extend into some of the dry rainforests of northern New South Wales and form a continuum with many of the vine thicket formations of the more arid inland.

The conservation value of these unique rainforests is worth examination. It is fortunate that some of the representative dune island rainforests have survived, despite the depredations of sand-mining and logging activities. The mainland littoral forests and thickets are less fortunate, and whereas at the turn of the century there was an almost uninterrupted strand of littoral forests and thickets along the east coast, there has been considerable fragmentation since, due to coastal development and extensive mining. It is not widely known that the littoral tracts are important migratory routes for many birds from both within and outside Australia. Furthermore, the littoral vegetation is an important buffer to coastal erosion and wind damage, and an important source of genetic material. These are places of quiet and intimate beauty which can give pleasure and inspiration to many.

Tropical rainforest rises above mangrove estuaries on Hinchinbrook Island.

THE RAINFOREST OF CHRISTMAS ISLAND

Many islands of the Great Barrier Reef, the Arafura Sea and Torres Strait possess fine stands of the 'drier' aspects of rainforests. Apart from these, the Australian nation has responsibility for the oceanic island territory of Christmas Island.

Christmas Island lies in the Indian Ocean approximately 360 kilometres from Java Head and 1408 kilometres from the nearest Australian point of North West Cape. It is about 132 square kilometres in area and at its highest point rises to 361 metres above sea level. Its chief importance to Australia is that it is one of our most important sources of phosphate. This is derived from the guano produced by the consolidated excreta of sea birds deposited over the millennia. There are no indigenous human inhabitants, most of the population of 3000 being concerned with the exploitation of the guano deposits.

The island experiences a seasonal climate with most of its annual rainfall of about 2000 millimetres falling between November and May. It has a unique rainforest with about 200 flowering plant species, of which about 15 are endemic. Despite the inroads from mining, this is one of the most intact, simply structured rainforests to be found anywhere in the world today, and it has some of the most remarkable fauna to be found in conjunction with rainforest. The island was formed as a coral limestone cap over an Eocene volcanic seamount and in most parts rises sheer from the sea with several flights of marine terraces, to an inland plateau. The plateau supports rainforest up to about 25 metres tall, with relatively simple structure and few tree species: *Planchonella nitida*, *Berria cordifolia*, *Eugenia gigantea*, *Ficus microcarpa*, *F. retusa*, *Hernandia ovigera* and *Tristiropsis nativitatis*. As well, there is a dense vine cover in many areas (*Hoya aldrichii* and *Schefflera elliptica*) combined with dense groves of *Pandanus nativitatis*. Epiphytes are common (*Asplenium macrophylla*) and ground ferns (*Bolbitis heteroclita*) and ground orchids (*Corymborchis angusta*).

Young red-footed booby in nest in *Gyrocarpus americanus* tree.

A particularly intriguing feature of the plateau rainforest is the close floristic relationship with shoreline species from the Indo-Malesian and Australian regions. Throughout the whole rainforest area are myriads of red crabs (*Gecarcoidea natalis*) which together with other plant-eating crab species (including the robber crab, *Birgus latro*) apparently act as a phytophagous sieve that controls the establishment of plant species on the island.

Christmas Island also possesses one of the most unique mangrove forests in the world. Whereas most mangroves exist in tidal conditions, the mangroves of Christmas Island are established on the old marine terraces about 40 metres above sea level, being fed

A buttress-rooted mangrove on Hinchinbrook Island.

by a freshwater spring. The main species is *Bruguiera gymnorrhiza* which is actively regenerating away from the sea, and with its own crab fauna.

It is the terrace forests below the plateau that are typical deciduous forests. These are up to 20 metres tall and are composed of many pantropic tree species that are found in seasonal deciduous forests of northern Australia (*Erythrina variegata*, *Gyrocarpus americanus*, *Melia azedarach* and *Terminalia catappa*). In some areas the forest is dominated by *Barringtonia racemosa* and *Pisonia grandis*. The main difference lies in the paucity of species in the Christmas Island deciduous forests. Although vines may be locally very dense, there are very few vine species, and quite often the forest takes on a park-like appearance with a clear floor that is due no doubt to the activities of the land crabs.

Robber crabs (*Birgus latro*) on Christmas Island.

Many sea birds nest in the rainforest trees, among them the noddy (*Anous stolidus*) and the incredibly beautiful golden bosun bird (*Phaethon lepturus fulvus*) which is straight from a fairy tale. Frigatebirds (*Fregata andrewsi* and F. *minor minor*) and red-footed boobies (*Sula sula rubripes*) also occupy the terrace forest. The world's largest booby, Abbott's booby (*Sula abbotti*) which is endemic to the island, unlike other boobies, nests in rainforest trees.

Because of high demand for phosphate which is a non-renewable resource, the mining program poses a real threat to the future survival of the island's unique flora and fauna. Fortunately, this has been anticipated to some extent, and there is now a national park established on the island together with a resident conservator. The Australian National Parks and Wildlife Service is at present seeking ways and means of conserving adequate stocks of wildlife and is actively promoting ecological studies so that adequate maintenance of the ecosystem is assured.

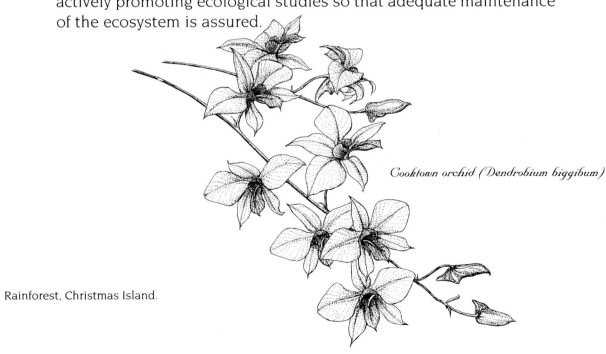

Cooktown orchid (*Dendrobium biggibum*)

Rainforest, Christmas Island.

END NOTES

THE CONTRIBUTORS

LEO MEIER has established himself as one of Australia's leading nature photographers. His technical expertise comes from a long training in printing, graphic arts, scientific and process photography. Although his photographic skills are wide-ranging, his profound affinity with nature makes nature photography his first love. His major nature publications have included *Australia the Beautiful Wilderness*, *Wilderness Blooms*, *Small Creatures of the Australian Wilderness*, *Daintree* and the outstanding recent publication *Australia's Wilderness Heritage*. Leo migrated from Switzerland in 1971 In the mid-1970s he began to lend his talent to the conservation movement in its struggles to preserve the Colo wilderness and the remaining rainforests. As a dedicated conservationist he sees his photography as the best way he can make Australians aware of the beauty and importance of their natural environment.

PENNY FIGGIS has been a campaigner for the Australian environment for 15 years. Like Leo Meier, she first became actively involved in the New South Wales battles to protect the Colo wilderness and remaining rainforests areas. In 1979 she obtained a first class honours degree in political science from Sydney University with a thesis on the environment movement. In the early 1980s she represented the Australian Conservation Foundation in Canberra as their national liaison officer. She has been a member of the board of management of Uluru National Park and has twice been vice-president of the Australian Conservation Foundation. In 1988 she was appointed a director of the Australian Tourist Commission to further the cause of environmental responsibility in the tourist industry. She is co-author of the 1988 publication, *Australia's Wilderness Heritage*.

DR AILA KETO was foundation president of the Rainforest Conservation Society of Queensland which was formed in 1982. She has written numerous articles on the values of, and threats to, Queensland's rainforests. Dr Keto was co-author of the report, 'A Study of the Conservation Significance of the Wet Tropics of North-East Queensland', which was commissioned by the Australian Heritage Commission. She was a delegate to the National Conservation Strategy Conference and the National Rainforest Conference, and is a member of the Commonwealth Rainforest Working Group charged with the task of developing a policy on rainforests for the Australian government. She is a Queensland councillor of the Australian Conservation Foundation.

DR KEITH SCOTT, a biochemist at the University of Queensland, has been actively involved in a number of conservation issues in Queensland over the past twenty years, both as secretary of the Rainforest Conservation Society of Queensland, and as convenor of the society's Rainforest Research Committee. Dr Scott was co-author, with Dr Keto, of the report to the Australian Heritage Commission on the rainforests of north-east Queensland.

ALLAN FOX trained as a teacher. He specialised in environmental education and social science. Transferring to the New South Wales Wildlife Service he became deeply involved in updating management and research processes of wildlife and its habitat. Later as the New South Wales National Parks and Wildlife Service's chief wildlife officer and education officer, and as chief of information and training for the Australian National Parks and Wildlife Service his work took him to many parts of Australia. In the Kakadu National Park, over a period of five years he came to know the monsoon forest intimately. Now, as an environmental consultant, he spends his time working on projects closely associated with the utilisation and conservation of the Australian landscape. He has written and illustrated a large number of articles as well as three successful books: *Together in Social Studies*; *Of Birds and Billabongs*; and *Australia's Wilderness Experience*.

DAVID ALLWORTH is Australian born. He has been closely involved with conservation issues since leaving school. He has worked in Sydney, Melbourne, Canberra and Brisbane for major conservation bodies. Forest conservation, especially rainforest conservation, has been a major interest. In the early 1980s he worked as the Australian Conservation Foundation's rainforest project officer. He has written numerous articles on rainforest conservation and is co-author of *Australian Rainforests: A Review*, published in 1982.

ALEX FLOYD, a research scientist with the New South Wales National Parks and Wildlife Service, has carried out an extensive evaluation of the rainforests of New South Wales, initially under secondment from the Forestry Commission of New South Wales, with whom he published a twelve-part series of booklets on New South Wales rainforest trees. His research has included the seeding, germination and regeneration of rainforest plants. He spent several years as forest ecologist in New Guinea.

KEVIN MILLS has undertaken research on the Illawarra rainforest vegetation for a Ph.D. thesis in the Geography Department at The University of Wollongong. He has carried out a number of other vegetation studies in southern New South Wales for the National Parks and Wildlife Service and other bodies. Other interests include a study of the rare plant species in the region, wetlands and their conservation and field ornithology, particularly of the rainforest birds. He is a keen bushwalker and

photographer, having contributed to a number of publications, and is co-author of the book *Native Trees of Central Illawarra*.

ROB BLAKERS developed a love for nature in the hills around Canberra, and in the Snowy Mountains. These feelings provided the motivation for four years of biology at the Australian National University. Since then, the attraction of the Tasmanian landscape drew out an intended four-week visit to become four years. For most of this time he worked on forest campaigns in Tasmania, and specialised particularly in the preservation of rainforest. He spent two years as 'Rescue the Rainforests' project officer for the Australian Conservation Foundation.

TIM O'LOUGHLIN studied biological science at Monash University in Victoria and has kayaked down many of Victoria's major rivers. He was involved in the campaign for a large alpine national park in Victoria. When he moved to Tasmania to kayak the Franklin, he became involved in the political campaign to stop it being dammed. Later he became forests project officer for the Wilderness Society. As co-director for several years of the Tasmanian Conservation Trust, he specialised in forest conservation issues.

DR ANDY GILLISON was born in Mackay, Queensland in 1937, and having spent most of his early years in far north Queensland, is no stranger to rainforests. Most of his working life has been spent in the rainforest and savanna environments of Australia and the south-west Pacific, with 16 years in Papua New Guinea, first as an agricultural extension officer and later as botanist and then forest ecologist. He is the author of a number of scientific papers on rainforest topics and several chapters in books dealing with Australian vegetation. He has attended a number of international expeditions to some of the more remote rainforests in the region and for many years has worked as a plant ecologist and a principal research scientist with CSIRO Division of Water and Land Resources.

ACKNOWLEDGEMENTS

Special thanks are due to Yvonne Cunningham and family and to Peter and Vince O'Reilly for the generous hospitality and advice they gave to Leo Meier while he was photographing for this book; to Clifford and Dawn Frith who wrote most of the captions; to John Benson for invaluable advice on many aspects of the book; and to Bill McDonald for reading and commenting on the manuscript.

The publishers would also like to thank the following for their generous help: David Allworth, Gregg Borschmann, Mark Broomhall, Mal Dibden, Milo Dunphy, Allan Fox, Rolf Gerig, Dr Andy Gillison, Mike Graham, Roli Haly, Carol Helman, Rosemary Hill, Dr Aila Keto, Sam Lewis Photographics and Staff, Greg Miles, Jane Moore, Ian Morris, J.A. Nieuwenhuizen, Val Plumwood, Pamela Seaborn, John Sinclair, Roger Smith, Colin Totterdell, Cliff Truelove.

PHOTOGRAPHIC ACKNOWLEDGEMENTS

Acknowledgement is made to the following for the photographs that appear on the pages indicated:
Rob Blakers: page 207; Bob Brown: page 208; Bob Burton: pages 213, 215; Peter Dombrovskis: pages 200, 203; Frithphoto: pages 22, 42, 53, 58, 62, 63, 76; Dr Andy Gillison: pages 233, 234, 235, 236, 237, 238, 239, 240, 241, 242, 257, 258, 259; Dennis Harding: pages 28, 210, 211, 214; David Heatley: page 209; Ern Mainka: pages 212, 218, 220, 221, 223; Colin Totterdell: pages 83, 86; A. Wapstra: pages 204, 205, 206.

PHOTOGRAPHIC NOTE

For the images in this book Leo Meier used Nikon 35mm cameras and lenses from 18mm to 600mm and Mamiya 6 x 7cm cameras with lenses from 50mm to 250mm. Films used were 35mm Kodachrome PKM and PKR and 120 Fujichrome RDP.